BUSINESS BASICS

MANAGING YOURSELF

How to achieve your personal goals in life and at work

Julie-Ann Amos

NICE WORK JONES.
YOU'RE IN FOR A
BIG PAY RISE!

How To Books

Author's dedication

To Peter, for his endless patience and proofreading. Chapter 5 may be of particular use when he realises how many of his suggestions I have ignored.

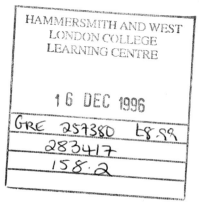

Cartoons by Mike Flanagan

British Library Cataloguing in Publication Data
A catalogue record for this book is available from the British Library.

© Copyright 1996 by Julie-Ann Amos.

Published by How To Books Ltd, Plymbridge House,
Estover Road, Plymouth PL6 7PZ, United Kingdom.
Tel: (01752) 202301. Fax: (01752) 202331.

Produced for How To Books by Deer Park Productions.
Typeset by PDQ Typesetting, Stoke-on-Trent, Staffs.
Printed and bound by Cromwell Press, Broughton Gifford, Melksham, Wiltshire.

3417

Contents

List of Illustrations

Preface

... for all those times we tried but tripped,
our hands held someone else's script.

R P Baker

We all want to live our lives in our own way. The problem is that so much of the time, other people, events and circumstances seem to manoeuvre us into situations in a certain way. We feel manipulated, controlled, helplessly stuck in our own lives and yet unable to make things happen the way we want. The secret lies in realising that we can't change other people. The answer lies in ourselves, and changing ourselves so we are ready to cope with all that life and other people throw at us.

This book gives you a variety of ways in which you can learn to manage yourself, and therefore learn to manage your life.

Each chapter concentrates on a different area, and there are questions and answers to help you understand the information. At the end of each chapter is a checklist, and discussion points to make you think about how what you have read applies to you. Finally, there are case studies in each chapter, showing three very different characters and how they cope with their lives – or don't!.

From all these, I hope you can learn to manage yourself, and start to find it easier to cope with people and situations that affect you.

Julie-Ann Amos

How good self-management can benefit you

Thinking positively

Receiving praise or criticism

Praising or criticising others

Calming angry or aggressive people down

Helping quiet, shy people to communicate

Standing up for yourself

Appearing helpful, cheerful and considerate

Getting the information you require

Getting answers to your questions

Dealing with your emotions appropriately

Expressing how you feel appropriately

Reducing negative feelings about yourself and others

Handling change

Being able to see other's point of view

Being reasonable

Letter others know they can talk to you

Behaving appropriately

Avoiding embarrassment

Communicating effectively

Making yourself understood

Checking you understand others

Handling stress

Negotiating with others

1
Motivating Yourself

Making things happen is one of the best ways to gain confidence. So why do we sometimes let others influence and control us to such an extent? Making things happen gives you confidence because:

• you feel effective

• you feel 'in control'

• you have a sense of direction and purpose

• you have a sense of achievement

• when things aren't going well, you can think back to past experiences to give you confidence to handle the present.

So, making things happen makes you feel good – it motivates you. Motivating yourself isn't always easy, but if you can understand how to get motivated, you can use those good feelings to help live your life as you wish. This chapter looks at some of the things that motivate people.

TALKING TO YOURSELF

Most people talk to themselves. Some are aware they are doing it, others aren't. But how many times a day do you **think** to yourself Thinking or talking, it's the same thing – you don't have to speak aloud. The inner conversations you have with yourself have as big an impact on your behaviour and your confidence as conversations you have with others. Maybe bigger. Imagine you are going to an important meeting. Your inner conversation might go like this:

Wrong	*Better*
'Oh no, I look a bit of a mess. I wish I had worn something else. And I've got a stinking cold. It's not a good day for me to be doing this.'	'Well, I may have a heavy cold but I'm determined not to let that show. And I've made an effort to look smart, which always makes a good impression.'

Which of these is going to make you behave and feel more confidently? It's obvious when you look at it like this, but it's surprising how much of the day we spend talking negatively to ourselves. If you could take all the time and energy you spend worrying and being pessimistic about things, and use it to plan how to cope with them and get them over and done with, you would feel and behave confidently, and probably achieve far more.

Nostalgia – revisiting the past

When we are worried about something, we often go back and look at how we have fared in the past. If your past experience is helpful, fair enough, but avoid going over old mistakes and failures – it achieves nothing, can lower our confidence and often makes us reluctant to persevere. Don't dwell on the past, especially if it's gloomy. Use the time to think about a better future.

Talking positively to yourself

Don't personalise

If people behave badly, or in a way you dislike, or that upsets you, don't take it personally. Just because someone ignores you, it doesn't mean they meant to, neither does it mean you aren't important. It just means they didn't acknowledge you. If people get angry with you, they are usually angry about **something**, not angry with **you** as a person. If you take things personally, it makes you insecure and makes it hard for you to be confident. Don't personalise.

Wrong	*Better*
'He doesn't like me'	'He's behaving rudely'
'She thinks I'm an idiot'	'She's treating me as if I don't understand her'

Don't exaggerate

Some people have a tendency to exaggerate, or dramatise what might happen. Don't. Even if bad things do always happen to you, talking about them won't help. Be realistic. Talking about things can often be a self-fulfilling prophecy. An old saying goes 'beware of what you wish for, because you might get it.'

Let go of the past
The past has gone. You have dealt with it – however badly – so move on and prepare for the future. And that doesn't involve dwelling on your mistakes. Talk future, not past.

Wrong	*Better*
'I handled that badly'	'I need to handle things better next time'
'I forgot what to say again'	'In future I need to remember to say...'

Separate who you are from what you do
Just because you do something silly, it doesn't make you silly. Doing something mean or petty, doesn't make you mean or petty. Separate **who you are** from **what you do** – you are not your behaviour.

Wrong	*Better*
'I'm stupid'	'I did something stupid'
'I'm clumsy'	'That was a clumsy thing to do'

ANALYSING MOTIVES

There are three main things that motivate people – that make people do things:

- they want to achieve

- they want to belong

- they want to influence.

You may be motivated by one of these, by two or by all three, but most people have one thing that is the strongest need. Here are some typical characteristics of each:

Needing to achieve

- aggressive or forceful

- always seeking ways to improve things

- difficulty relaxing

- easily bored

- energetic

- enjoy challenges

- fear of failure

- find it difficult to work hard if work is routine or unstimulating

- frustrated when let down or delayed

- look for feedback on own performance

- set goals and deadlines

- take responsibility

- tend to talk about success, failure, effectiveness, results, outcomes, etc.

Needing to belong

- avoid being direct

- avoid conflict

- concern with creating relationships

- enjoy liaising or discussing with others

- favouritism

- fear of rejection

- feel that people and relationships take priority

- like people

- seek social contact

- tend to talk about reputation, recognition, influence, contacts

- worry how people see you.

Needing to influence
- enjoy associating with powerful and influential people

- enjoy being assertive and influencing people

- fear of loss of status or control

- feel that reputation and status are important

- good at mobilising and organising others

- like making things happen using other people

- take control of situations

- tend to dominate others

- tend to operate using favours granted and received – the 'old boys network'

- tend to talk about relationships, emotions, feelings, opinions, etc.

Take time to think about what motivates you, and what motivates the people around you. Sometimes, differences in motivation may explain why you and someone else never seem to 'see eye to eye'. If you can see where they are coming from, you can often see how to approach them better – how to deal with them. Talk to them on their own terms; persuade them in their own language.

QUESTIONS AND ANSWERS

So should I stop talking to myself?
No. Talking to yourself (either aloud or thinking to yourself in your head) can be very effective in giving yourself confidence. Just follow

the golden rules: talk and think positively, not negatively; don't dwell on the past – look forward to the future; accept your weaknesses, and concentrate on your strengths; be optimistic, not pessimistic.

How does my motivation help me deal with others?

If you can see what motivates someone, you can see how best to communicate with them in a way they will understand. Let's look at an example. Assume you are motivated by achievement, your partner is motivated by belonging, and your child by influence. If you want to go on holiday to Scotland to learn to ski, that would fulfil your need to achieve, to have a challenge. But the thought of learning to ski isn't a motivator for the others. You could best persuade them in their own terms. Show your spouse (who needs to belong) how taking a holiday would mean spending time together, and socialising. Show your child (who needs influence) how you and their friends would be impressed if they learnt to ski, and how they could be one of the first at school to learn. Explaining things like this is far more likely to appeal to them.

I don't always feel motivated. How can I feel more enthusiastic about the things I have to do?

Just as you can appeal to what motivates someone else, you can appeal to your own motives. It won't always be possible, but maybe you can see value in something if you think about it differently. If you are motivated by achievement, try making lists of jobs to do, and ticking things off as you do them. Even small boring tasks will be an achievement – a tick off the list. If you are motivated by belonging, try discussing things with others for ideas or opinions. Or try to work with others, to do things quicker in return for helping them. If you are motivated by influence, keep track of ways in which you can assist others, or of people you can use for advice or information (this is called 'networking'). Keep a record of useful information, and always be on the look-out for opportunities to impress – not to 'suck up' to people, but to let them know what you're capable of.

SETTING STANDARDS

We all set our own standards. We have an inbuilt set of standards and rules by which we live. This is similar to what motivates us, but subtly different. The thing that motivates us, encourages us to do

things. The standard we live by dictates **how** we do those t.
These standards are sometimes called **drivers**. Being **motiva** ..
positive, being **driven** is not. Being motivated is something we
choose, being driven means we have no choice – something in us
drives us to behave in a certain way, regardless of whether it is
pleasant or appropriate for the situation. There are things driving
most people – standards built into them which they have to live up
to, not by choice, but because it is part of their personality.

There are five drivers, or standards. Psychologists say that these
are developed by people when they are very young, as a way of
pleasing and getting on with others. We then keep the standards
inside us for the rest of our lives, like a set of rules we live by. Not
living up to our inner standards can be frustrating, stressful and
irritating, making us feel bad without knowing why. Which of the
following five drivers is the most important to you?

Speed – the standard of the hurrier

You may have an urge to hurry. Do you do things at top speed,
getting a great deal done – often more than most people could do in
a similar amount of time? Do you feel good doing things in the
shortest possible time? Do you spend time thinking of better and
faster, more efficient ways to do things? If so, you could be a hurrier,
living your life by the standard of speed. This has a number of
advantages, but unfortunately, it also has disadvantages.

Advantages of hurriers
- Don't miss deadlines.

- Efficient.

- Good achievers.

- Need little time for preparation.

- Quick-thinking.

- Work well under pressure, against the clock, with tight deadlines.

Disadvantages of hurriers
- Impatient, and pressurise others.

- In haste, mistakes can be made.

- Quick thinking often leads to quick talking, and interrupting, and not listening to others.

- Rushing too much to be on time for things.

- Things can be missed or not checked properly.

- When there is plenty of time, things often get put off until they become urgent.

Perfection – the standard of the perfectionist

You may have an urge to be perfect. Do you like everything to be exactly right? Do you hate making mistakes? Can you always find something wrong if there's something to be found? If so, you could be a perfectionist.

Advantages of perfectionists
- Accurate.

- Don't make mistakes.

- Have contingency plans for potential problems.

- Reliable.

- Well organised.

- Well presented.

Disadvantages of perfectionists
- Can be so detailed it confuses or irritates others.

- Can be slow, as checking every detail takes time.

- Critical.

- Fear of making a mistake may lead to hesitation, or even doing nothing.

- Often end up not trusting others to do anything to the required standard.

- Poor at meeting deadlines, as emphasis is placed on quality, not quantity.

Approval – the standard of the pleaser

You may have an urge to gain approval. Do you try to please people without them asking? Do you feel very hurt by criticism? Are you good at listening and understanding others? Do you always try not to rock the boat? If so, you could be a pleaser.

Advantages of pleasers
- Good at smoothing things over.

- Good listeners.

- Intuitive – can see how others are feeling and thinking.

- Kind and considerate.

- Understanding.

- Well liked.

Disadvantages of pleasers
- Can cause misunderstandings due to acting on intuition, instead of checking facts.

- May not tell others even when you know they are wrong, in case you upset them.

- May be seen as weak, due to reluctance to put forward own ideas and opinions.

- Reluctant to say no, so can get overloaded.

- Take criticism too personally.

Effort – the standard of the trier

You may have an urge to try hard. Are you hard-working? Do you put a lot of effort and enthusiasm into things? Do you often volunteer? Are you bored by detail? Are you easily distracted by new things? If so, you could be a trier, living your life by the standard of effort.

Advantages of triers
- Enthusiastic.

- Thorough – look at all the possibilities and options.

- Well motivated.

- Work hard.

Disadvantages of triers
- Can turn simple tasks into major ones because of enthusiasm.

- May start things but not finish them.

- May volunteer for too much, becoming over-committed.

- More concerned with effort than success – therefore may not succeed very often!

Strength – the standard of the coper
You may have an urge to be strong. Do you stay calm under pressure? Do people come to you for help and support? Are you even-tempered and consistent? Are you always reliable and dependable? If so, you could be a coper, living your life by the standard of strength.

Advantages of copers
- Don't over-react.

- Don't panic.

- Deal calmly with angry, upset or difficult people.

- Good at dealing with difficult or stressful situations.

- Good in a crisis, when others panic.

- Honest.

- Predictable.

- Reliable and steady.

Disadvantages of copers
- Afraid of letting people down.

- Can be hard to get to know, because feelings are covered up.

- Can get overloaded, because never seek help themselves.

- Hate admitting weakness.

- See failure to cope with everything as a weakness.

Motivation and drivers

Can you see how combinations of the three needs and the five drivers can combine to make us the way we are? For example, if we are motivated by achievement, our driver will dictate exactly **how** we try to achieve. Hurrier achievers will try to achieve as much as possible, as quickly as possible. Perfectionist achievers will try to achieve things as well as possible. Pleaser achievers will try to achieve what other people want. Trier achievers will try to take on as much as possible, but can end up in a bit of a conflict, as they may end up not achieving much. Coper achievers will try to achieve whatever is required, even when others can't or don't. The other motivators and drivers lead to other combinations.

ACCEPTING REALITY

The most important thing is to be realistic. You want to do things because you are motivated, but you are driven to do them in a particular way, to a particular standard. Try and work out what the standard is, and stop to ask yourself some tough questions. Is doing it this way appropriate? Does this **have** to be perfect? Do I **have** to cope with this alone? Do I **have** to finish this by tomorrow? Set your own standards, and try to relax them to a reasonable point when possible. Here are some ways you can be realistic within your standards.

Realistic hurrying
- Allow enough time to do things properly.

- Check things and don't make assumptions.

- Concentrate on listening to others.

- Plan enough so you avoid mistakes.

- Try not to interrupt.

- Try consciously to slow down when dealing with other people.

Realistic perfectionism
- Don't swamp people with a mass of information they may not need.

- Finish things on time, even if they aren't perfect.

- Prioritise, so you can see which things really are important enough to warrant 100 per cent accuracy.

- Set deadlines so you don't get bogged down with checking and rechecking details.

- Think of mistakes as a method of learning how to do better next time.

- Try to relax more and accept that nobody (including yourself) is perfect.

Realistic pleasing
- Accept that being realistic isn't letting others down, it is being honest with them.

- Learn to say 'no'.

- Set your own priorities and standards – don't try to do things to other people's.

- Try to be assertive.

Realistic trying
- Be self-disciplined – get on with things whether they are exciting or not.

- Don't allow yourself to become bored with things you have started.

- Set deadlines for all parts of a job, so things get finished as well as started.

- Try to find ways to make routine, boring tasks interesting.

Realistic coping
- Check what is involved before taking responsibility.

- Don't be afraid to ask for help when you need it.

- Learn to say 'no'.

- Look out for weaknesses which you may have hidden from yourself.

CHECKLIST

- Be aware of how and when you are talking to yourself, either aloud or in your head. Try to keep what you are saying positive, realistic and optimistic.

- Be aware that other people's motivations are not always the same as your own.

- Try to talk to people in their own terms – try to see what motivates them and talk to them in those terms.

- Try to keep assessing situations, to make sure your behaviour is appropriate.

- Try to be reasonable and realistic. Drivers sometimes push us so far into one way of behaving that we lose sight of the facts and the situation.

CASE STUDIES – AN INTRODUCTION

Let me now introduce you to three fictional people whose lives we will be observing in the following chapters. Each is different, and deals with situations in their own way. Any resemblance to real individuals is entirely coincidental. We will observe how each of these characters handles a variety of situations, and how their own decisions and actions affect themselves.

Julia Norris, librarian

Julia Norris is librarian of a small library in a country village. She has three part-time staff working for her, and has to deal with a variety of visitors to the library. She prides herself on being efficient and organised, and likes to think that she is always fair, open-minded and assertive, both at work, and at home with her husband and two teenage children.

Paul Haines, barman

Paul Haines is a young barman in a large, busy, city-centre public house. He often has to deal with high-spirited and unruly customers, and needs to be able to take charge of the situation at times. He admits he has a 'short fuse', but prides himself that he never hits anyone, and is good at 'sorting things out'. He feels that he is in control and assertive, although he does admit that friends and others have said he makes them nervous at times.

Erica Lawson, secretary

Erica Lawson is secretary to an ogre of a divisional director in a large retail company. She tries always to do her best, and supervises one typist, which she feels she does well. However she often feels anxious, even undermined at work, because of her boss's overbearing attitude. She feels she cannot stand up for herself more, and do herself justice, because she is only a secretary, and others in her division (who are all professionally qualified) usually know far more than she does. She therefore feels unsure of her facts or even her opinions at times. She is newly married, and would like to have a baby.

DISCUSSION POINTS

1. What motivates you most? What motivates you least?

2. Try to think how much each of the five drivers affects you. Which is the most influential on how you behave? Which is the second most?

3. How could you be more realistic, and not let your drivers drive you to behave in ways which are not always appropriate?

2
Praising and Criticising

Most of us like to be praised, and hate to be criticised. It's important to appreciate how to give and receive praise, compliments and criticism, to avoid embarrassment to either party. First, let's look at criticism.

GIVING CRITICISM

If you don't give criticism when you should, you run the risk of two things going wrong. Firstly, you may leave it too late to deal with the problem effectively, and secondly you may leave it so long that you become frustrated and over-emotional, and then deal with the matter too forcefully. Remember you can't change others, only yourself, so concentrate on dealing with issues in the best possible way. That way, it gives the other person maximum opportunity to deal with the matter reasonably.

Reactions to criticism
There are four main reactions:

- acceptance
- partial acceptance
- failure to take responsibility
- denial.

It would be nice if people accepted our criticism, but be prepared for only a partial acceptance, or for a complete denial. Or they may accept the facts, but deny it was **their** fault – they may try to shift the blame.

Criticising effectively

Ask permission
Ask the person's permission to talk to them – don't just hit them

with the bad news. If they have agreed to have a conversation, they are more likely to be listening, and therefore receptive to what you are saying. It minimises the chance of their mind being elsewhere.

Be constructive

Criticism without offering advice or an alternative way to do things is called destructive. Helpful criticism, with advice on what to do to put things right, is called constructive. So, don't just tell people what they've done wrong, also tell them how to put it right. It would be wrong just to criticise and not offer any suggestions as to how to improve – it just isn't fair. You may not have to offer advice – maybe they will see what needs to be done themselves, but always be prepared to point out what they can do.

Be effective

Don't criticise someone when they aren't listening. Don't criticise if they're not in the right frame of mind either, if possible. If you say your message while they aren't prepared to hear it, they either won't take it in, or they may misinterpret what you are saying.

Be factual

Remember that when we looked at talking to yourself in Chapter 1, we saw how you need to separate yourself from your behaviour. Well, help others to do the same. Criticise them in a way that criticises their behaviour – **what** they have done, not **who** they are. Don't say 'you're messy', or 'you're thoughtless'. These aren't criticisms, they're huge labels you are attaching to the person. What you really mean is that they have made a mess, not that they are a messy person. Or, you mean that they have behaved thoughtlessly, not that they are thoughtless all the time. So say what you mean, in factual, not personal terms.

Be focused

Don't criticise a whole load of things in one fell swoop. Only deal with one matter at a time if possible, unless there are several examples of the same thing which you can raise. Even if there are, you don't have to raise them all – just mention enough to prove the point, then let the others drop. Raising too much at once is overwhelming.

Be honest

So often we exaggerate something to make it seem more important.

If it's important enough to deal with, deal with it – without exaggerating it. If it isn't, then let the matter go, and don't criticise every trivial little thing. Exaggerating issues is dishonest, and if you do it often, it may lead to serious facts being dismissed as exaggeration – 'crying wolf'.

Be open
Don't tell people to change – remember, you can't make them. Just **ask** them to do things differently, and be open to their efforts.

Be positive
Before you launch into telling someone what they have done wrong, try to find something they have done right which you can also mention. This balances the conversation, and makes them more likely to listen seriously to your point. It also means they are less likely to get defensive and reject your criticism, or take it too much to heart, and get upset.

Be prepared
Prepare a little script of what to say if necessary, but at least know your facts and be prepared for resistance, or upset. If you are prepared well for all eventualities, you are less likely to be thrown if things start to get difficult.

Be private
Never criticise people in front of others if at all possible. They will resent it, and either become defensive, or over-upset. It can be both humiliating and damaging.

Be realistic
There is little point in asking people to do something they can't. So be realistic in what you expect. Don't expect them to respond to your criticism overnight. Set a realistic target for what they need to do, and by when.

Be receptive
Let the other person have a say – criticism needn't (and shouldn't) be one-sided.

Be specific
If you are general about things, people can't relate to them – they can't see exactly what needs to change. Be specific wherever

possible. If people don't understand exactly what is wrong, they are less likely to be able to put things right. Tell them exactly what is wrong, and offer suggestions as to what they can do to put it right. Often, people are sensitive about being criticised, and will say they agree and understand even if they have no idea what you mean. So spell it out for them – nicely.

Be sympathetic but firm
Listen to the other person, but stick to your guns if the criticism is justified.

Be timely
Don't wait too long before dealing with issues. Waiting too long trivialises the matter, and the other person may forget about it.

RECEIVING CRITICISM

Reacting to criticism
Remember the four reactions to criticism? Well, make sure you listen carefully to the criticism, and then choose your reaction.

Acceptance
If criticism is founded in fact, and you are responsible, then accept it graciously.

Partial acceptance
If part of the criticism is fair and founded in fact, accept that part only, and make it clear you don't accept the rest.

Failure to take responsibility
If the criticism is of something that isn't your fault, but was caused by another party, you have the option to take responsibility yourself and then deal with the other person afterwards, or not to take responsibility. For example, if a manager criticises a piece of work which you submitted but which was done by someone else, you could choose to say it wasn't your work, or equally, you could accept the criticism and then take the matter up with the person who did do the work. Use your own judgement.

Denial
If criticism is untrue or the facts are wrong, say so. There is no need to argue, just state the truth calmly and logically.

Dealing with criticism you accept

Be balanced
When someone is criticising you, try to keep a balanced view –
remember you have good points too! This will stop you getting too
depressed about what is being said.

Be calm
Try to stay calm, so you can discuss things rationally and not
emotionally.

Be receptive
Few people like being criticised, but you should welcome
constructive criticism, as a means of finding out how you can
improve. Criticism is just information about ourselves, after all, and
information about how others see us is useful.

Be specific
You're being criticised for something you've done, not for who you
are. It's important to remember this, as many people criticise badly
– we are used to being labelled. Accepting a label about who we are,
instead of what we've done, often upsets us or makes us defensive.
So even if the other person is labelling us, try to remember it is
really what we did that is at fault, not our person.

Deal with exaggeration
If the criticism is founded in fact but has been exaggerated, ignore
the exaggeration. Then accept the part of the criticism that is true.
Pointing out the exaggeration just means a confrontation – a
difference of opinion, which can lead to argument. So acknowledge
and accept the truth, and ignore the exaggeration.

Don't get defensive
Being defensive and snapping back at someone usually leads to an
argument, and that isn't a sensible way to achieve anything. Instead,
be assertive – later chapters will show you how.

Don't be submissive
Don't just give in and accept criticism. If it's unfounded or incorrect
or unfair, say so. Say you disagree. You don't have to start an
argument, just state your own side of things clearly and calmly.

Question if necessary
If you don't understand what is being raised, say so. Ask for clarification. Or, if you don't see where the criticism comes from, ask for specific examples. If the criticism seems very personal, ask why the comments are being made.

Thank them
This is hard – thank the person for pointing out the things they have raised. This is important, as it lets them know you are approachable.

Use facts, not emotions
Don't get emotional, or talk in emotional terms. This will help the other person not to get emotional, either, and keep things on an even keel.

QUESTIONS AND ANSWERS

I don't always find it easy to tell exactly what is being criticised – it all seems petty and trivial. Should I really bother with it?
Vague criticism can be questioned. But some people say things that sound like criticism, but are really not. These statements may just be 'dampeners', or 'put-downs' – things designed to make you feel bad, and/or make them feel better. Such things include back-handed compliments, where a criticism is disguised as a compliment. If you are the subject of such nasty comments, don't get emotional. Tone of voice is very important, as if you stay calm and reasonable, the other person's unreasonable comments will be highlighted. Just think what the hidden message is, and ask them whether that is **really** what they mean. For example, if someone says 'typical woman', try asking, 'do you mean I am feminine, or were you criticising women in general?'

Is it important to deal with criticism and put-downs?
Yes. Put-downs are a form of aggression, where someone tries to feel better at your expense. They are using you in a way that makes you seem inferior. Criticism should also be dealt with. If it's fair, you need to tell the person you have taken their points on board, or they may raise them again. If it isn't fair, you should stand up for yourself politely. This will give you confidence for the future.

GIVING PRAISE AND COMPLIMENTS

It is important to give praise and compliments when appropriate, as this is one of the things that give people confidence. Most people are boosted and encouraged by praise or compliments. Yet some of us find them difficult to give, as we feel embarrassed, or think we will sound insincere.

Be honest
People will sense a false compliment, and it will cause friction. Only give genuine praise and compliments – don't fib.

Be specific
Saying 'you did really well' is nice, but can sound insincere, and doesn't help the person know exactly **why** or **how** they did well. Try 'I really liked the way you did x...'. It makes the compliment sound tangible – it gives them something concrete and specific to feel good about.

Don't put yourself down
Don't talk about yourself and the person you are complimenting at the same time. To compliment others by contrasting with your own (poor) performance or ability makes it difficult for them not to feel awkward, whereas a compliment is supposed to make them feel good. Give them the compliment in their own right, not as a measure of how they compare with you.

Keep your tone light
Compliments sound insincere if they are said too enthusiastically. Just state the compliment clearly and nicely – don't over-do it!

RECEIVING PRAISE AND COMPLIMENTS

Receiving compliments can be embarrassing. We all like praise, but something in us makes us shy, and we handle it badly. This can take some of the pleasantness away.

Don't argue
If someone compliments you, don't argue with them. It's easy to say, 'no, it was rubbish!' This sort of comment just makes the complimenter feel silly, and discourages them from saying nice things again.

Don't question them
It's tempting to say, 'what, this old thing?' or, 'really, why on earth do you say that?' Questioning them is rude, and makes them feel

bad. They don't have to justify saying something nice.

If you are suspicious, question
Okay, so sometimes you have that sneaking suspicion that the person isn't really serious, but is making a point. In that case, ask them what they mean. If they are being devious, it will become apparent. If it was a genuine compliment, just accept gracefully.

Say 'thank you'
Just say 'thank you' after a compliment. You don't need to say anything else. It will make the giver feel good, and encourage them to make compliments again.

CHECKLIST

- Give criticism and compliments promptly – both are reduced in their impact if they take place too long after the event.

- Criticise properly – bad criticism leads to arguments and emotional responses.

- Don't personalise, either when giving or when receiving criticism.

- Choose your reaction to criticism – don't get caught up in reacting instantly, think and choose how you want to react.

- Be gracious about giving and receiving compliments.

CASE STUDIES

Julia deals with criticism from her manager
Julia has an appraisal once a year with her area manager. This year, a number of areas which needed improving were raised. Julia didn't feel some of the points were her fault at all. 'Thank you for being so honest,' she began, 'but I'm not clear why you're raising some of these things with me. Staff training and the book circulation rotas are really outside my control. Is there anything I'm missing in these areas? I feel I've made a good recommendation, but surely that action now rests with the support group?' It emerged that Julia's manager was under the impression that she hadn't dealt with these issues, not that she was waiting for action by others. He agreed to help Julia push things forward, and accepted it wasn't her

responsibility. Julia's approach was far better than getting defensive, with a 'that's not my job!' approach.

Paul clashes with some customers

A party of businessmen came into the bar at 4.30 one Friday afternoon. They became noisier and noisier, and by 8.00 p.m. Paul decided enough was enough. 'You're drunk and out of order!' he declared flatly when they next came to order more drinks. 'If you don't sort yourselves out, I'll have to ask you to leave.' 'Who's drunk?' one demanded, 'We're just having a good time!' 'You're noisy and rude,' Paul replied, 'and I'm warning you!' 'Come on lads,' the other man said, 'let's leave Killjoy here and go somewhere better!' Paul had wanted to change their behaviour. Instead, he criticised what they were – a personal label, almost guaranteed to make them defensive. Also, he never pointed out what action he wanted – 'sort yourselves out' is a bit vague! He should have focused on what they did, not criticised who they were, and he should have been constructive.

Erica diverts praise and rubbishes herself

Erica's typist finished a long complex report. When Erica gave it to the Director, he said, 'Erica, this is excellent! Thank you so much for your effort – I'm impressed, as I know you're busy today.' She was surprised – he didn't usually show appreciation for her work, so to cover her confusion she said, 'Oh, it wasn't me actually. Joanne did it. It would probably have taken me ages longer – I'm hopelessly bogged down at the moment.' She acknowledged the true deserver of the praise, but in doing so, she reinforced her boss's negative opinion of herself. She should have said something like, 'Thank you. I'll pass that on to Joanne, as I delegated this to her.' It keeps her in control of the situation, without taking the credit from Joanne.

DISCUSSION POINTS

1. Listen to people criticising and praising. How could the points raised be rephrased to come across better?

2. Think about when you are criticised. How do you tend to react? Do you get defensive? Upset? Think of ways you could react better.

3. Practise giving short, simple compliments to others. Notice how they handle them, and learn from their reactions.

3
Handling Thoughts and Feelings

Thoughts and feelings aren't the same. Have you ever noticed that? A **thought** is 'I'm miserable!' A **feeling** is feeling miserable. It may or may not cause us to behave miserably, but **behaviour** is something different as well (see Figure 1). The important thing is that feelings don't just happen – they're caused. And if they don't just happen, that means we can do something about them: people and things that happen don't *make* us feel the way we do, we can control how we feel, at least to some extent.

Fig. 1. Thoughts, feelings and behaviour.

Some feelings are good. We probably don't mind being happy, excited, proud and so on: these are **positive feelings**. What most people would prefer is to get rid of feeling angry, depressed, upset, sad, etc. – **negative feelings**.

HANDLING NEGATIVE FEELINGS

When we are experiencing negative feelings, there are two main things that most people do:

1. We keep them suppressed – bottle them up and behave differently from how we feel (**suppression**).

2. We let them out with our behaviour (**expression**) – are angry, sad etc.

In this way, we let feelings dictate our behaviour. This isn't really good for us. Feelings are important – they do matter – but they shouldn't dictate how we behave, even how we live our lives.

Suppressing negative feelings
Suppressing feelings can lead to all sorts of trouble:

- depression

- emotional withdrawal

- low self-worth

- psychosomatic illnesses

- resorting to drugs or alcohol.

The problem is that feelings are like energy – they're the energy that was designed to fuel your behaviour. So when you keep that energy pent up inside for too long, and don't release it, you become like an over-cooked stew, bubbling away in the oven. Eventually, because you can't keep the energy held in for ever, one of three things will happen:

- you can't keep it all in, and eventually boil over anyway, ending up expressing what you wanted to keep hidden, *or*

- you get over-cooked, and spoil – you make yourself ill, *or*

- the energy leaks out gradually, in abnormal behaviour – nailbiting, overspending, gambling, drinking, over-eating, under-eating, etc.

So suppressing negative feelings isn't the answer.

Expressing negative feelings
Unfortunately, this too can get you into trouble:

- lost tempers

- sulking

- sarcasm.

The problem is that when we start using the energy, letting it out, we can lose control. We can release too much – our behaviour can be excessive. What we need to do is to express our feelings **appropriately** – so others around us are less likely to feel uncomfortable.

Expressing negative feelings appropriately

There are three main ways to do this:

- before you lose control

- during loss of control

- after loss of control.

Remember 'talking to yourself' in Chapter 1? This is where it can help. When you feel negative feelings, remember Figure 1 – the feelings are caused by thoughts. Before you reach breaking-point, stop and think. Nobody's saying it's easy, but stop and ask yourself **why** you are feeling like this. There must be a reason.

Example
Someone pushes in front of you in the supermarket queue. You feel anger. Why? What thought caused the feeling of anger?

'Why didn't the cashier stop them?'
'How rude!'
'Now I might be late!'
'How dare he?'
'Why did I let that happen?'

Well, deal with the thought, not the feeling, before the feeling of anger is expressed. Express the thought, not the feeling. Later in the chapter you'll see how to verbally express the feelings, by **negative feelings assertion** – you don't have to say nothing. But first, deal with the thoughts and see if the anger drains away.

Thought	*How to express the thought*
'Why didn't the cashier stop them?'	You're actually feeling angry with the cashier and expressing it to the other customer will therefore serve no purpose. You need

to tell the cashier that the incident made you angry (see later in this chapter for how to say this) and say that you think they should have done something about it.

'How rude!'

You're feeling angry because the other person has behaved rudely. Will getting angry with them make them less rude? Probably not. You need to decide whether you want to say anything, or just to accept that they have behaved badly.

'Now I might be late!'

You're feeling angry because you think you may be late. Will being angry make you less likely to be late? Of course not. You'll be late or you won't, and feeling happy, sad, angry or relaxed won't make any difference. So being angry in this case is pointless. If you want to raise the subject with the other customer, however, you could.

'How dare he?'

You're feeling angry because you think the other person has belittled you. They are behaving as if you are 'less than' them. Does their behaviour mean you're less important? Of course not. If anything, their behaviour shows **they** are less considerate than **you**. You could mention it to them, or to the cashier, but the cashier can't do anything about it, so you would only be letting off steam, not achieving anything, and technically, mentioning it to someone not responsible is just grumbling.

'Why did I let that happen?'   You're feeling angry with yourself
                               for not stopping the person.
                               There's no point expressing anger
                               to other people when it's against
                               yourself. You need to use what
                               you read in Chapter 1 – talk to
                               yourself. OK, so you let some-
                               thing happen you shouldn't have
                               done. Well, it's too late now, so
                               think about how you'll handle it
                               next time.

Some people will think it's a waste of time standing there thinking
about **why** you're feeling angry. But consider that while you're
thinking about why you're feeling angry, you're not letting your
thoughts generate more anger. You're distracting yourself – not
focusing on the anger, but on the cause.

Thoughts aren't the only thing that will help, however. A good
way of expressing feelings is to say something. This technique is
called **negative feelings assertion**.

NEGATIVE FEELINGS ASSERTION

Negative feelings assertion is where you express your negative
feelings verbally. I know that just saying you're angry or upset
doesn't sound as if it will stop you **feeling** angry or upset, but you'd
be surprised. After all, why do you behave in an angry or upset way?
So people know you're angry or upset, of course! So if you **tell** them
you feel angry, for example, you don't need to **behave** angrily as well
– they'll get the message without you shouting at them.

Telling people how you feel is actually quite hard for a lot of
people – most people don't do it very often. However, it can prevent
your feelings from bursting out and telling them how you feel in a
far more unpleasant way. Which would you rather have – someone
telling you they feel upset, or someone bursting into tears? Express
the feelings in calm words, not in uncontrolled behaviour.

Four steps
There are four steps in negative feelings assertion. Take another
look at Figure 1 – the four boxes. All you have to do is to explain
each of them.

Step one – Explain the event
Say what the person has done – how they have behaved.

Step two – Explain the thought
Say how that affected you.

Step three – Explain the feeling
Say how you feel.

Step four – Explain the behaviour
Say how you would like them to behave.

Sounds simple, doesn't it? Let's go back to the supermarket, and go through each of the thoughts you might have had and see how to use negative feelings assertion to express your feelings.

Examples of negative feelings assertion

Thought – 'Why didn't the cashier stop them?'

To – the cashier
1. (event)   'When that customer pushed into the queue in front of me...'
2. (thought)   '...I thought you should have said or done something about it...'
3. (feeling)   '...It made me quite angry...'
4. (behaviour) '...In future, I'd appreciate it if you wouldn't serve people out of turn.'

Thought – 'How rude!'

To – the other customer
1. (event)   'When you push in front of people who are queuing...'
2. (thought)   '...I think it's very rude...'
3. (feeling)   '...I feel angry...'
4. (behaviour) '...Please be more thoughtful/considerate...'

Thought – 'Now I might be late!'

To – the other customer
1. (event)   'Because you have pushed in front of me...'

2. (thought)   '...I think I may be late...'
3. (feeling)   '...and I'm getting angry...'
4. (behaviour)   '...Please be as quick as possible or move to the
                  back of the queue.'

Thought – 'How dare he?'

To – the other customer
1. (event)   'When you push in front of other people...'
2. (thought)   '...it implies you feel superior to them...'
3. (feeling)   '...That makes me feel angry...'
4. (behaviour)   '...Please don't push in front of me again.'

Thought – 'How dare he?'

To – the cashier
1. (event)   'When people push in front of me...'
2. (thought)   '...I feel very belittled...'
3. (feeling)   '...and angry...'
4. (behaviour)   '...I wish people wouldn't do it.'

Remember in this case, the cashier isn't the cause – they are just a
bystander, and mentioning it to them may make you feel better, but
it's really just grumbling – you might as well tell anyone!

So, by expressing our negative feelings in a calm, reasonable way,
after thinking things through properly, we can deal with our feelings
without suppressing them.

QUESTIONS AND ANSWERS

*Surely doing all this would just take so long that the situation would
have blown over before I get to work out what to say?*
Perhaps so at first, but with a little practice, you will think faster and
learn how to respond to events and express your feelings at the time.
And don't forget, just by thinking things through, you aren't
concentrating on your negative feelings, and so they are less likely to
overwhelm you.

Should I always tell people how I feel?
No. In some cases, as in some of the examples we've looked at, it
wouldn't achieve anything. You may well think there's no point in

saying something if it will make the situation worse. However, saying how you feel gets it out in the open, and can sometimes make you feel a lot better. Even if nothing will result, there's no harm in saying how you feel if it will help you feel better.

I feel silly saying 'I feel angry' – it sounds so emotional doesn't it?
We aren't used to people saying how they feel – we're more used to people telling us how they feel by their behaviour, and expecting us to translate that behaviour into an awareness of what's going on inside them. But the behaviour is often unpleasant for the people around us. It would be far better just to say how we feel, without using the behaviour.

BOUNCING BACK

Dealing with things is all very well if it goes according to plan. But what happens if you say your piece and the other person still behaves badly towards you? Or, if you can't deal with the matter for some reason, so you can't defuse your feelings? Or maybe after dealing with it, you still don't feel any better. This section is about trying to pick yourself up and bounce back after experiencing negative feelings.

Stay flexible
Just because you wanted things to work out in a certain way, if they don't there's no point in persisting with your way of dealing with things. Accept the way things are going and work on dealing with that – don't stick to your original thinking when the situation changes.

Focus on results
Don't focus on what happened or how you did or didn't deal with it. Just concentrate on the result – the outcome, and coming to terms with that. If you dealt with something badly, don't waste time thinking about the original situation, or how you handled it. Concentrate on how you feel right now and how to get those feelings positive, rather than negative.

Look for a benefit
I'm not saying talk yourself into thinking things are all right, but if something has turned out in a particular way, try to see a benefit or advantage to that. This will help you to get your feelings more

positive. For example, if you handled something badly and lost your temper, and now feel guilty, try saying to yourself, 'I handled that badly. However, at least I got the anger out of my system. I did it inappropriately, it's true, but now I have got rid of it, perhaps I can talk to the person again and put things right.'

Don't feel a compromise is a loss

If you deal with a situation and feel unhappy with the result because it didn't turn out the way you would have liked, this doesn't mean you lost. A compromise is where both people adjust their wants so they can accommodate each other. Coming to a compromise doesn't mean you didn't win. It means you unselfishly helped the other person, and they did the same. Think of it like that and you may feel better. Some people call this a 'win-win' situation.

CHECKLIST

- Separate how you feel from what you think. Events don't cause feelings, they cause thoughts, which in turn cause feelings.

- Don't suppress negative feelings – it can make you ill and cause more problems than expressing them.

- Express negative feelings appropriately. That means calmly, and without letting them take control of you.

- Practise **negative feelings assertion** to tell people how you feel by using your words, and not your behaviour.

- If you still have negative feelings after using **negative feelings assertion**, try to bounce back and help yourself to feel more positive. Avoid dwelling on what happened.

CASE STUDIES

Julia faces an angry customer

Julia was called to the library desk to deal with an angry customer. He explained he had telephoned to renew his books, but now he was being fined because they were late. 'I'm telling you, I renewed them!' he said angrily to Julia. 'I'm sorry, sir,' she replied, 'but the computer definitely says these are overdue. There's £1.75 to pay.' 'You can forget that!' he shouted. 'I'm not paying any fine! I

renewed them and *you* messed it up! You're all the same, you lot –
sat about in here all day – nothing better to do than make a fuss
about a few pence. If you'd done the job properly, the computer
would be right, wouldn't it?' He glared angrily at Julia, and
thumped the books down on the counter.

She took a deep breath, and concentrated on speaking calmly to
him. She ignored the comments about herself, and concentrated on
the problem. 'I can see you're very angry,' she began. He snorted
and folded his arms. 'It makes me think that either you believe we're
dishonest, or you genuinely *meant* to renew the books, and believed
you had done. I feel upset that you're angry at the staff for the error,
and would ask you to calm down, so we can discuss this. The
computer definitely shows the books overdue. The fine may only be
a few pence, but the library service **is** free, and books are very
expensive nowadays. I hope you understand.' He was obviously still
unhappy, but reluctantly agreed to pay the fine.

Julia effectively used negative feelings assertion to point out that
he was upsetting her by criticising the staff.

Paul loses his temper
The same businessmen reappeared in the bar the following Friday.
They sneered at Paul, calling him 'Killjoy' and laughing at him. Paul
got more and more angry. Eventually, his short fuse got the better
of him, and the anger that had been brewing came out. 'Why don't
you grow up?' he called across the bar. They just laughed at him,
and he felt even more angry. When they left, he stormed round the
bar all night, and everyone noticed his ill-humour.

The manager had to speak to him about it, as Paul had been
barely civil to the customers. By this time Paul had had enough, and
he had an angry argument with the manager – obviously not a good
thing to do with your boss!

Paul needs to learn how to express negative feelings appropriately,
so they don't end up being expressed in an uncontrolled way.
Uncontrolled expression isn't pleasant – for you **or** other people,
and it can result in trouble, as Paul discovered when his manager
gave him a warning for his outburst.

Erica is angry with herself
Erica hadn't had a good week. The Director had been finding fault
with everything, and she had been running around looking for
various mislaid items. He kept interrupting her with queries and
urgent but trivial tasks, and her work was piling up. Instead of

saying something, she suppressed all her frustration.

The last straw was at 5.00 pm, when he called her in to return all the correspondence she had prepared for him to sign. A whole day's correspondence was useless – she had dated it next year, not this year! She had been interrupted so many times, and working under such pressure that she must have overlooked it.

She felt humiliated – it was such a stupid mistake. So she added anger at herself to the boiling pot of negative feelings stored inside. When she got home, she tossed and turned all night and couldn't sleep. The next day, she had visitors and another sleepless night. On Sunday, she felt as if she hadn't slept for a week, and she dreaded going in to work early on Monday to re-do Friday's correspondence. She was well on the way to being ill from suppressed negative feelings.

If she could have expressed at least **some** of her frustration, she would have felt better, might have been able to sleep, and even her selfish boss might have had a little more sympathy.

DISCUSSION POINTS

1. Think of the last time you experienced strong negative emotions; for example, when you got angry, or frustrated. Who was it with? Think about how you could have expressed those feelings appropriately, telling them how you felt, using negative feelings assertion.

2. When someone is expressing negative feelings to you by using behaviour (for example, getting upset or angry), think of ways in which you could help them express those feelings in a way that would be more pleasant.

3. Do you suppress negative feelings? Try to think which feelings in particular you suppress, or with whom you suppress negative feelings. Try to think of ways in which you can express these, so you don't keep them bottled up.

4
Understanding Behaviour and Assertiveness

IDENTIFYING BEHAVIOUR

How we behave reflects how we feel. To simplify behaviour, imagine you only have two feelings – you feel good or you feel bad. All feelings come under those two headings only. You could either feel good about yourself, or bad about yourself. Whenever you come into contact with another person, you either feel good or bad about them as well. This means there are only four combinations of feelings:

1 Feel good about self Feel other person is good	3 Feel bad about self Feel other person is good
2 Feel good about self Feel other person is bad	4 Feel bad about self Feel other person is bad

Don't worry about **why** you feel like this, just think about people you interact with and how you feel about them. These four combinations are likely to influence our behaviour. If you look at box 2, you feel good, and feel the other person is bad. This means you are likely to behave in a superior way – you feel you are better than them, more important. Similarly, in box 3, you feel the other person is better than you, so you are likely to behave in a subservient or passive way.

These four boxes help explain why you sometimes behave the way you do. The behaviour usually linked to the feelings in the boxes is shown in the chart over the page.

So, for example, if you tend to be aggressive, it is often because you feel others are 'less than' you in some way – less important, less

	Feel good about self	Feed bad about self
Feel other person is good	ASSERTIVE BEHAVIOUR	PASSIVE BEHAVIOUR
Feel other person is bad	AGGRESSIVE BEHAVIOUR	DEPRESSIVE BEHAVIOUR

able, less knowledgeable, etc. Similarly, if you tend to be passive with someone, you probably feel 'less than' them in some way. This book concentrates on the three main behaviours – assertiveness, aggressiveness and passivity. The fourth – depressive behaviour, is just as it sounds – depressing. People who feel like this usually don't see the point in trying to change – they feel bad about themselves, and they feel everyone else is no better, so no one can help them. They probably wouldn't read this book.

UNDERSTANDING ASSERTIVENESS

The dictionary has several definitions of assertiveness:

- 'claiming your rights'
- 'declaring strongly'
- 'insisting upon'
- 'standing up for yourself'.

One dictionary lists it as 'making aggressive claims or statements' which really doesn't describe assertiveness at all well.

Assertiveness is about how you express yourself. It means being aware of:

- what you need from others
- your opinions
- what you want
- how you feel, and
- what you believe.

It means expressing the above things:

- appropriately
- calmly
- clearly
- directly
- honestly
- in a way that helps others remain calm
- in a way that allows both you and others to keep your dignity or pride
- without violating other people's rights.

ANALYSING YOURSELF

So, how can you tell how assertive you are? Here are some of the signs of assertiveness. See how many of them apply to you.

Identifying assertiveness

☐ Asking, not telling.

☐ Asking questions to check you understand.

☐ Assertive body language (see Chapter 7).

☐ Being brief – not rambling.

☐ Being clear.

☐ 'Being yourself'.

☐ Calm, neutral tone of voice.

☐ Criticising constructively.

☐ Deciding **not** to be assertive if you don't wish to.

☐ Eye contact – looking at who you're talking to.

☐ Expressing your own thoughts, feelings, opinions, etc.

☐ Stating, not lecturing.

☐ Knowing your opinions, feelings.

☐ Making suggestions, not giving advice (unless asked for).

☐ Not apologising excessively.

☐ Not feeling guilty without reason.

☐ Not interrupting.

☐ Not labelling people – separating their behaviour from who they are.

☐ Saying 'no' without feeling guilty or selfish.

☐ Speaking at a sensible speed – not too fast, not hesitating.

QUESTIONS AND ANSWERS

I always thought that being assertive meant behaving aggressively – getting what you want, being forceful, etc. Isn't that right?
No. Dictionary definitions don't help misunderstandings, but there are many reasons why people get confused. Assertiveness comes from a feeling of equality – that both you and the other person/ people are good, that you have equal rights, and equal value. That's quite rare. If you were brought up in an environment where you were taught always to be polite and considerate, you may see ordinary assertiveness as aggressive. If you equate passiveness with politeness, you may equate assertiveness with aggression. You may think that going along with other people is being helpful. But assertiveness is about being honest – about saying what you think and feel, in a polite and considerate way.

I think I'm probably not assertive because I don't feel equal to others a lot of the time. Surely this means I can't ever be assertive?
Not at all. We saw earlier that events cause thoughts, which cause feelings, which cause behaviour. But in reverse, if you choose to behave in a certain way, your feelings can often change. So for example, if you feel very shy and embarrassed, but decide to behave naturally and try to overcome it, often you will start to feel more confident as your feelings come into line with your behaviour. Similarly, if you feel angry but try to behave calmly, the anger may start to subside (if it doesn't get worse for not being expressed!). If you try your best to behave assertively, as you get used to it and see what effect it has on others, it will affect you – giving you more confidence and making you feel more good about yourself and others.

Are aggressive, passive and depressive behaviour bad, then?
Any behaviour is bad if you do it because you have no choice – if
it's a **reaction** you can't control. Often, our feelings and moods come
flooding out when it might be better if they didn't. If you **choose** to
behave aggressively, or to be passive once in a while, fine. The
problem comes when you behave like that because 'it's the way you
are', rather then because you choose to. You can't be more in
control of your life if you can't even control your own behaviour.
The right behaviour for you is the behaviour you **choose** – not the
behaviour your emotions cause. Later you will see how to **respond**,
(which means choosing your behaviour) – not just **react**.

DEVELOPING ASSERTIVENESS

Remember this book is about what **you** can do to make things
happen. What you can't do is change other people. Assertiveness is
like planting seeds. They may grow, they may not, but by planting
them and looking after them and making all the conditions as
favourable as possible, you've got the best chance of things turning
out as you would like. So, how do you be assertive? There are lots of
ways, but to start with, let's look at handling situations. It would be
nice if you could simply learn a script of what to say in each
situation, and say it when appropriate, but there are far too many
situations and factors to allow this. What you *do* have is a basic
formula, which you can remember by using the word **PLANT**.
Figure 2 explains this.

USING PLANT

PLANT is a blueprint you can follow to help you structure what to
say in difficult situations. One thing it does is take your mind **off**
what is happening, how you feel and are reacting, and focus your
thoughts onto how to respond. Just that change of emphasis from
being **in** the situation to thinking **about** the situation will help you to
stay calm and in control. If you are interrupted, just go back to **L**
and start listening again. Listen to the interruption, acknowledge it,
then keep going. Here are some ways to handle specific situations,
with do's and don'ts to help you stay assertive.

Making requests

Do
● Be brief.

P	**PREPARE** in advance. Unless the situation arises without warning, prepare how you will handle it. Go through the other 4 steps and decide how you could handle things assertively. Think how to deal with potential problems. Decide exactly what you want to achieve. Even if you are surprised by a situation, you could always ask to discuss it later, giving you time to prepare.
L	**LISTEN** actively to the other person and what they have to say. Make sure you've understood by asking questions if necessary.
A	**ACKNOWLEDGE** what they have said. *Tell* them you have understood. This is vital, to make the other person listen and not interrupt. People often interrupt because they think you haven't understood, and they're more likely to listen to *you* if they know you listened to *them*.
N	**NOW IT'S YOUR TURN** to put across clearly, calmly and concisely what you want to say, your opinion, how you feel, or the facts as you see them. This is where you get to make your own point.
T	**TRY TO AGREE**. Lastly, indicate what you want, and try to come to an agreement or compromise. At least show you are willing to go on and discuss the issue. Then let them speak and start listening again.

Fig. 2. Assertiveness.

- Be direct.

- Be open.

- Believe you have every right to make a request.

- Give a brief reason for the request.

- Respect their right to say 'no'.

- Make sure they know you respect it.

Don't
- Apologise for asking.

- Beat about the bush.

- Butter people up with flattery.

- Exaggerate to make it sound more important.

- Manipulate people into saying 'yes'.

- Play on your friendship or relationship.

- Plead.

- Refuse to take 'no' for an answer.

- Take refusal personally (this is one of the things that makes it difficult for people to say no).

- Threaten.

Saying 'no'

Do
- Acknowledge the request and their right to make it.

- Ask questions if you need more information before making a decision.

- Be brief but not curt.

- Be honest – try to give the real reason for refusing, even if it's 'I don't want to'.

- Personalise your decision – don't hide behind rules and other people.

- Say it nicely!

- Take your time – often people resent an instant refusal, but if you take time to think about it and then say 'no', they accept it.

Don't
- Apologise unnecessarily.

- Be abrupt.

- Believe that if you refuse, you won't be able to make requests in return.

- Feel guilty.

- Make excuses.

- Think you have no right to refuse.

- Worry they will be hurt.

- Worry they will stop liking you.

Dealing with people who won't take 'no' for an answer

Do
- Keep to your original decision to refuse.

- Make sure you use the word 'no' – check you actually **say** it, not just imply it.

- Simply repeat your refusal, adding your reason if you didn't give it.

- Stay polite.

Don't
- Be swayed from your decision.

- Become impatient.

- Repeat your reason if you have already given it.

- Start questioning your own judgement.

- Think of more (better) reasons.

Disagreeing with people

Do
- Accept that you have every right to your own opinion.

- Be firm.

- Be honest.

- Be open-minded – you could be wrong.

- Be polite.

- Realise that an opinion isn't right or wrong, it's just someone's opinion.

- Separate facts from opinions.

- Stick to logic, not emotion.

Don't
- Apologise for disagreeing.

- Be afraid they will get angry or upset – they are responsible for their own feelings.

- Dismiss what they have said as useless, not worthwhile, etc.

- Get caught up in 'point-scoring'.

- Gloss over differences.

- Put the other person down.

- Say nothing.

- Use emotional terms – I hate it, I love it, it's foolish, etc.

AVOIDING THE PITFALLS

There are many reasons why people find it hard to be assertive. Here are some of the main ones.

Concentrating on the person
People have power over us because we focus on **them**, rather than on the situation. Everyone is equal, so focus on the situation and you will be less intimidated by people.

Lack of clarity
You may have confused ideas, thoughts, emotions, standards. You need to spend some time deciding exactly what you **do** want, think, feel about some things. If you don't know what you want, how on earth can you ever hope to get it? If you don't know what you think, how can you put it across? If you don't know how you feel, you are at the mercy of all those feelings, which may make you behave in a way you don't have control over.

Lack of practice
Because you aren't used to being assertive, it may well be difficult at first, and seem like a lot of time and effort for little result. Practice not only makes it easier, it also makes you more likely to have a positive outcome.

Lack of self-confidence or self-respect
If you don't feel good about yourself, it's hard to be assertive. Do try, however, as changing your behaviour can lead to a change in how you feel. Accept that you have rights and they are equal to other people's – we're all equal. The old saying 'treat others as you'd like to be treated' is a very good one. If other people have the right to polite treatment, so do you. If they have the right to say 'no', so do you.

Not knowing your rights
Everyone has rights. Here are some of the main ones:

- to ask for what you want

- to change yourself if you want to

- to change your mind

- to express your opinions and feelings

- to make decisions and choices

- to make mistakes

- to privacy

- to say 'no'

- to your own opinions

- to your feelings.

Suppression of emotions

If you suppress emotions, they may come out unexpectedly. If you express them appropriately (assertively), they will be 'defused', and less able to affect your behaviour.

RESPONDING NOT REACTING

The goal is for you to **choose** your behaviour, and not to be at the mercy of your feelings – not behaving in a certain way because your emotions give you no choice. What you need to do is to **respond**, not **react**. A reaction is something that happens just because something else does – cause and effect. A response is a chosen reaction. The ability to respond and not react means having our emotions, thoughts and behaviour all under control.

Why do I react in a certain way?

There are many reasons, including:

- because it's expected of you

- because of habit

- because the other person is reacting

- because you are afraid

- because you can't think what else to do

- because you don't feel good about yourself

- because you don't know what's happening

- because you think you have no choice

- because you feel confused or trapped.

How to respond

To respond and not react, first you have to stop yourself reacting. Consciously don't do anything. Then think – what was I just about to do? Why? Do I want to do that? If you do, fine. If not, you need some thinking time. There's nothing wrong with saying, 'Can I think about this for a minute?' to someone. Then think about it, and decide what you **want** to do. This is responding.

The main problem is **time**: it all takes time. This is why using **PLANT** to be assertive helps. You buy time while listening to the other person, asking questions if necessary. You also slow things down by acknowledging. Then you can ask for more time if you need it, and say what you want to say calmly. You can't guarantee it will work all the time, but it's better than being at the mercy of your instant reactions.

CHECKLIST

- Understand what assertiveness is, and don't confuse it with aggression.

- Check your own behaviour for assertiveness. Try to increase your assertive behaviour.

- Learn to use **PLANT** for tricky situations.

- Respect both your own rights and those of others.

- Practise assertive behaviour, which may impact on your emotions, making you feel more assertive as a result.

- Respond, don't react. Don't be afraid of time – you are entitled to time to think about things before responding.

CASE STUDIES

Julia listens carefully and responds assertively

Julia's assistant Angela arrived at work one day, obviously excited. She had been asked to go on holiday with her boyfriend's family. The problem was, the library was already short-staffed for that week.

Julia dealt with it assertively. First, she listened carefully to Angela, and then said, 'That's wonderful, Angela. I can see how excited you are. *My* difficulty is that I already have two people on holiday that week, so I can't confirm that you can have the time off unless I can get cover from another library. I *will* try, but until I'm sure, you have to realise I can't guarantee you the time off.' Angela pleaded with her. 'I understand, and I *will* do my best, but I can't guarantee it.' Julia repeated.

She had every right to say 'no', under the circumstances, but offered to help in the way she could, without giving in.

Paul's manager says 'no', but fails to explain fully

There was a birthday party at the bar. Paul stayed late, and the usual arrangement was that he be paid overtime, but when he received his payslip, there was no extra pay. He spoke to the manager, who explained, 'I missed the cut-off date, sorry.' 'Can't you pay me in cash?' Paul asked. The manager shook his head. 'No, I'm afraid not. It'll be on next week's slip.'

Paul was cross, and felt aggrieved – he thought the manager should have paid him in cash for the overtime. Worse, he'd promised to treat his girlfriend to a meal with the money. He was determined not to go out of his way to help the manager again.

Later, he found out from one of the other staff that the manager usually paid extra cash from the petty cash box. 'That's it!' Paul said, 'I'm going to have it out with him!' The manager had been abrupt when he said 'no', not explaining fully why he couldn't give Paul the cash.

After Paul had burst in and made his point, the manager explained that the petty cash had all been used up on extra decorations for the birthday party. Had he explained that, he could have avoided the friction between himself and Paul. As well as avoiding the unpleasantness, Paul would have accepted that he couldn't have the cash, if he had known the reason.

Erica's fails to say 'no' clearly

Erica was also asked to work overtime. She couldn't, because her mother was in hospital and she had already needed to visit her several times that week. On the evening in question, she had promised to babysit her sister's two children, so her sister and her husband could visit her mother. However, she didn't like saying 'no' to her boss, who could be very insensitive at times.

'I'm really sorry,' she explained, 'but I'm not sure that I can.' 'Can you find out and let me know?' he asked without even looking up. 'Well, it's my Mum, you see – she hasn't been well,' Erica continued, 'I'm really sorry, but it's probably pretty unavoidable, really.' 'So you can't?' he asked, looking up. 'Well, not really, I'm sorry,' Erica said, feeling very uncomfortable, 'you see I said I'd babysit...' 'I thought your mother was ill?' he interrupted. 'She is, but the thing is, I said I'd babysit for my sister, so *she* could visit...' Erica continued. 'OK, forget it!' he interrupted crossly.

What an unpleasant man! But Erica didn't really help herself. There was no way she could work, but when he asked her, she didn't actually say 'no' – she just kept apologising and explaining! She was weak and wishy-washy, and her reason sounded like a feeble excuse – no wonder he grew impatient. She should have said 'No, I'm sorry – I already have commitments.' Short and honest. If he wanted to know exactly why, he could have asked. She sounded as if she might change her mind, so he tried to pressure her into doing so. She needed to be more firm.

DISCUSSION POINTS

1. How many of the signs of assertiveness do you regularly show? Think of ways you can work on using more of them.

2. Think of five situations which might arise which you would like to deal with assertively. Go through **PLANT** and write out a script for the imaginary conversation, to deal with the issues.

3. Why do you sometimes find it hard to be assertive? Is it with certain people? Over certain issues? Under certain circumstances? Is your lack of assertiveness really reasonable, or are you reacting out of habit, or because it's expected of you? How could you react differently?

5
Handling Aggression

Aggression isn't a pleasant behaviour. We need to know how to deal with it when we start to behave that way ourselves, or when others are behaving that way towards us.

EXPLAINING AGGRESSION

Dictionary definition
The dictionary lists aggression as:

- unprovoked attack

- the urge to show hostility

- threatening behaviour

- being quarrelsome, etc.

Signs of an aggressive viewpoint
Remember the boxes in the last chapter? Aggression comes from a mental viewpoint of feeling good about yourself, and bad about others – that you're 'better than' or 'of greater value than' others in some way. Aggressive viewpoints include:

- believing others do not have the same rights as you

- believing your own wants/opinions/needs/feelings are more important than others'

- expressing your own wants/opinions/needs/feelings in an inappropriate way

- ignoring the wants/opinions/needs/feelings of others

- standing up for your rights in a way that violates others'

- standing up for yourself in a way that puts others down

- winning a situation at the expense of others.

Why become aggressive?

There are two reasons why anyone behaves the way they do:

1. Lack of control (reaction)	2. Choice (response)

Being aggressive works the same way – we are aggressive because we do not control our behaviour, and **react**, or because we choose to be (**respond**).

Reactive aggression
Uncontrolled aggression can be due to:

Attack – an in-built defence mechanism for some people is to respond with aggression when you are attacked, or think you are being attacked, or even when you predict you might be attacked.

Release – releasing suppressed feelings in an uncontrolled manner, such as a loss of temper – 'the straw that broke the camel's back'. Remember, suppressed feelings usually come out sometime, and often in the form of uncontrolled aggression.

Responsive aggression
Choosing to be aggressive can be because:

- you are retaliating for the past aggressive behaviour of others

- you think that aggression will get the result you want

- you are, or have been in the past, encouraged to be aggressive.

IDENTIFYING AGGRESSION

How many of the following signs of aggressive behaviour do you recognise in yourself?

- Boasting – 'I'm always on time', 'I finished that last week', etc.

- Describing behaviour in emotional terms – 'that was stupid', 'what a crazy way to do it', etc.

- Expressing opinions as facts – 'You can't do that', 'It won't work', etc.

- Giving unsolicited advice – 'You ought to...' 'Why don't you...' etc.

- 'I' statements, indicating self-centredness – 'I'd like', 'I think', etc.

- Lecturing.

- Making assumptions – 'I don't suppose', 'I assume you haven't...'.

- Nagging.

- Phrasing requests as orders or threats – 'I want you to...', 'You'd better...' etc.

- Putting people on the spot.

- Sarcastic comments – 'Don't be stupid', 'Not if I have anything to do with it', etc.

- Threatening use of questions – 'What did you do that for?', 'Who said you could?' etc.

- Unconstructive criticism – criticising without indicating how things can be put right.

EXPERIENCING THE EFFECTS

The effects on you
In the short term, aggression may get you what you want. Or if it doesn't, you may at least feel a release of tension as you express your feelings, and a sense of power and control over the situation. These feelings are good. The problem is that after these go, you are left with any or all of the following bad feelings about having been aggressive (see also Figure 3):

- defensive – always waiting for someone to attack you

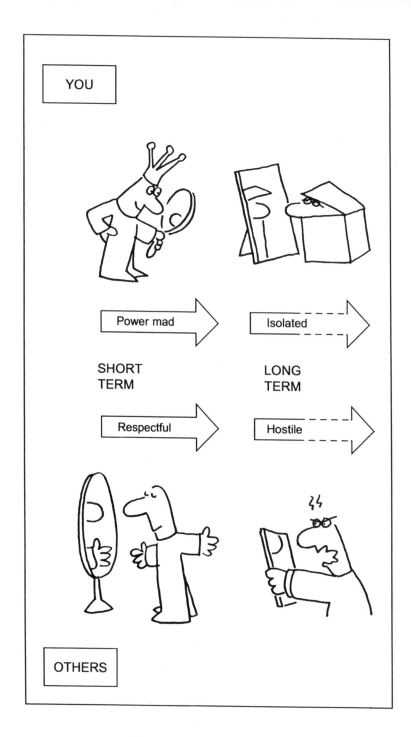

Fig. 3. The effects of aggression.

- drained of energy

- embarrassment or shame over behaviour

- emotional turmoil

- guilt over behaviour

- isolation

- relationship problems – lack of trust of/from others

- tendency to blame others for your outbursts.

The effects on others
In the short term, you may be admired or respected for speaking out. But mostly, people feel:

- afraid

- angry

- frustrated

- humiliated

- hurt

- rejected.

QUESTIONS AND ANSWERS

I thought expressing our feelings was a good idea; shouldn't aggression be expressed as well?
Suppressing feelings is bad for you, generally speaking. Expressing them is better, as long as you find a way of expressing them **appropriately**. The problem is, aggression tends to be difficult to express appropriately. The following pages will help you deal with aggression you experience.

I can recognise aggression in others, but I don't see it in myself until I lose my temper and explode. Why?
You are probably experiencing reactive aggression. You suppress it until it finds a way to release itself, and suddenly you lose your temper. If you suppress it well enough, you forget it's there at times,

but the anger and negative feelings *are* there, building up and ready to burst out when provoked. It's like stamp collecting – you collect your stamps in a little mental book, until you have enough to trade them in for an outburst – just like collecting the old 'Green Shield Stamps'.

DEALING WITH AGGRESSION

When people are aggressive towards us, it is often unpleasant. There are three ways in which we could behave in return – aggressively, passively or assertively. The natural tendency is to **react** instinctively, which usually means aggressively or passively. Few people naturally and instinctively react assertively. For most of us, assertiveness is a **response** rather than a reaction – something we must consciously try to do. We need to practise the assertive response, especially when dealing with aggression, because it generates strong feelings in us – most, if not all of them, negative ones.

Reacting to aggression with aggression – PLANT
This situation is likely to escalate into argument or unpleasantness, with both people trying to win or gain advantage at the expense of the other, due to their viewpoint of the other as 'less than' themselves in some way.

Reacting to aggression with passivity
This will bring a temporary relief from unpleasantness, but suppressing your feelings leads to trouble, as has already been said.

Responding to aggression with assertiveness – PLANT

Preparation
- Firstly, remember that the person's aggression may not actually be directed at you. They may be angry with themselves, with others, or with circumstances – it's just that they are **expressing** it at you. Remembering this may help you not to take things personally, and get upset or defensive.

- Deal with the instant reaction of thoughts and feelings that well up inside you. Try to be objective and sensible about how the aggression is making you feel – try to keep things in proportion.

Listen

- Listen to what they are saying – just the words. Ignore the unpleasant behaviour, sarcasm, aggressive tone of voice and all the other things that aren't part of the **content** of what they are saying. Just concentrate on listening to the words, and deal with the meaning of those only. You probably don't like their behaviour, so just ignore it.

Acknowledge

- Firstly, acknowledge that you realise they're angry. And that doesn't mean saying things like 'Calm down!' Say something neutral such as 'I can see you're angry/frustrated about this,' or 'You're obviously angry/frustrated.' Such neutral statements do two things. Firstly, they highlight the other person's behaviour, which is important because they may be so wrapped up in how they feel that they don't even realise they are doing it! Second, if the point of behaving aggressively is to give you a message, let them know you've got it! Your underlying message here is, 'Look, I know you're angry/frustrated, so there's no point in going on *showing* me – I've got the message.'

- Secondly, acknowledge what they've just said. But whatever you do, **don't** acknowledge the way they said it – remember, ignore the unpleasant parts of their behaviour, and focus on the content.

Now it's your turn

- Expect to be interrupted. Aggressive people do it a lot – and they usually can't see what's wrong with doing it, as they feel they have a **right** to speak. Interruptions disrupt you far less if you expect them.

- Put your own message across calmly and concisely. It is important to be calm because they are already enraged, and you want them to calm down, not get worse. Be concise, because it gives them less opportunity to interrupt, and if they **are** listening, they will get more frustrated by long-windedness. Be as short and to the point as you can.

- Expect to have to repeat yourself, as they rarely listen properly to you. This could be because they feel they don't have to – remember their viewpoint is that you are 'less than' them. But also, when someone gets angry, the effect of the hormones and chemicals that are released into their bloodstream is to reduce the amount of oxygen getting to their brain. In short, they *can't* listen properly – it takes a while for things to sink in with a very angry person, as their brain's reactions slow down. So, be patient.

Try to agree
• Tell them what you'd like to happen.

• If they really are behaving in a way that's difficult to cope with, try suggesting that you discuss this at a later time – maybe setting a time and date so they can see you aren't just 'putting them off'. This will give you time to prepare, and give them time to calm down. Also, there isn't any point in discussing things if they are too emotional to be constructive and sensible.

Sounds simple, doesn't it? In the face of aggressive behaviour, it is difficult not to react to it, but what will achieve most is to think carefully and choose our response, to put ourselves and our points across as effectively as possible.

CHECKLIST

• Always remember that aggressive behaviour isn't necessarily about shouting and waving your arms about. It's *any* behaviour with a viewpoint of 'I'm better than' or 'you're less than'.

• Be aware that aggression may make you feel good in the short term, but is never good for you in the long term.

• Always respond to aggression by keeping assertive – remember **PLANT**. It may not work first time, but seeds take time to grow!

CASE STUDIES

Julia experiences aggression from a customer
A customer came into the library to complain that she had been waiting for a reserved book for three weeks. Julia explained there was nothing that could be done until the book was returned. The customer suggested that a search be made to see what had happened to the book. She also suggested that the procedure for reserving books be altered to operate more efficiently. She also insisted on spelling the long words in the book title for Julia.

When the customer left, Julia sighed. 'What an aggressive lady!'

she remarked to one of the staff. 'Oh, I thought she sounded polite. ' the colleague answered. Julia explained that treating others as if they are less intelligent than you, and offering unwanted advice, is aggressive. It indicates you feel superior, and prevents them from feeling equal.

Paul's aggression provokes an aggressive reaction

Paul took Saturday off, and was having a quiet drink with his girlfriend in another bar when a couple of teenagers started making sarcastic comments. 'Let's leave,' his girlfriend suggested. 'Wait a minute,' Paul replied, and went over to give the lads a piece of his mind. He told them to watch it, pointing at them with his finger. Instead of letting him go, they stood up and one of them shoved Paul. The situation quickly became very argumentative, which is exactly what happens when you react to aggression with aggression.

Erica puts up with more criticism from her boss

Erica was having a party. She invited her boss, but he didn't come. On the morning after the party, he made a number of comments about her work – insinuating indirectly that it was slow because she had been up revelling for half the night. 'Sorry,' she said, 'I didn't realise I was taking so long. Perhaps I'll work through the lunch hour.'

The problem with being passive and not handling the situation assertively was that her boss didn't realise that her party was to celebrate the fact that she was pregnant. No wonder she wasn't at her best in the mornings!

She should have been assertive, and said something like, 'It isn't the after-effects of the party, actually. I'm going to have a baby, and I feel a little unwell some mornings. Perhaps you could understand and be a little patient on days when I feel out-of-sorts?' Even if he was unpleasant and no better after her conversation, at least she would have felt better for making her point instead of feeling guilty for something that wasn't really her fault.

DISCUSSION POINTS

1. How many of the signs of aggression do you see in yourself?

2. Do you get aggressive with certain people? In certain situations? Over certain issues? Try to establish a pattern (if there is one) to your aggression. It will help you prepare to be more assertive.

3. How does aggression from others make you feel? What can you do to overcome this?

6
Dealing With Passivity

We saw in the last chapter that aggression is pretty unpleasant behaviour. But passivity isn't much better, either in ourselves or in others. You need to know how to deal with it effectively in others, and how to recognise and start to work on passive behaviour in yourself.

EXPLAINING PASSIVITY

Dictionary definition
The dictionary definitions of passivity include:

- a state where action is suffered by the subject

- being acted upon, but not acting

- inactive

- submissive

- unresisting.

Signs of a passive viewpoint
Again, think back to the boxes in Chapter 4. Passivity comes from a mental viewpoint of feeling bad about yourself and that others are better – that you're 'worse than' or 'less than' others in some way. Passive viewpoints include:

- aiming to please others and avoid conflict

- being apologetic and diffident

- believing others have more rights than you

- believing others' wants/opinions/needs/feelings are more important than yours

- believing you have little or nothing to contribute

- not standing up for yourself and/or your rights.

Why become passive?

As with aggressive behaviour, there are two reasons why people behave passively – reaction or response.

Reactive passivity
Reacting passively can be because of:

- belief that you are 'less than' others, or

- fear of negative consequences – of anger, upsetting the other person, of being penalised, etc.

Responsive passivity
Choosing to be passive can be because:

- you believe passivity to be polite and/or helpful

- you want to avoid behaving aggressively

- you were brought up to behave passively.

IDENTIFYING PASSIVITY

How many of the following signs of passive behaviour do you recognise in yourself?

- Apologising excessively.

- Dismissing your own wants and needs – 'it doesn't matter', 'I don't mind', 'I'll manage' etc.

- Hesitation words – 'um', 'er', 'you know', 'I mean', etc.

- Justification of your actions.

- Putting yourself down – 'I'm useless at . . . ', 'I don't think I can . . . ' etc.

- Rambling – long complex explanations.

- Saying nothing.

- Self-directing – 'I must', 'I should', etc.

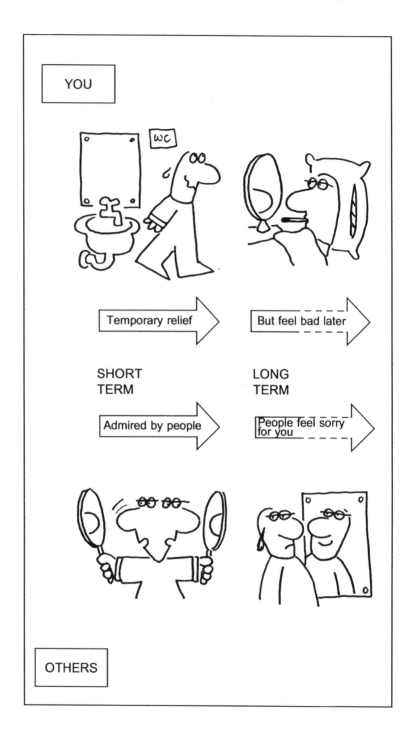

Fig. 4. The effects of passivity.

- Seeking permission – 'would you mind if?', 'can I?' etc.

- Using qualifiers – 'maybe', 'perhaps', 'I can't be sure', etc.

EXPERIENCING THE EFFECTS OF PASSIVITY

The effects of passivity on you
In the short term, passivity may bring a temporary relief from tension and/or anxiety. Also, you may feel relief that you have avoided guilt or confrontation. You may even feel good – proud or pleased with yourself, for being so 'nice'. These feelings are good. The problem is that just as with the effects of aggression, after these go, you are left with any or all of the following bad feelings about having been passive:

- depression

- feeling angry or frustrated with yourself

- feeling hurt, or sorry for yourself

- feeling used – like a 'doormat'

- guilt over being dishonest

- loss of self-esteem

- possible psychosomatic illnesses

- recognition that you are unable to tackle difficult situations

- self-pity.

The effects of passivity on others
In the short term, you may be admired or respected for 'keeping the peace', but people are more likely to feel sorry for you. Mostly, people feel:

- embarrassed

- frustrated

- guilty for taking advantage

- irritated by your passivity

- lack of respect for you

- lack of trust

- sorry for you.

QUESTIONS AND ANSWERS

So, isn't being passive better than being aggressive?
They're both harmful in the long run. People find passive behaviour easier to deal with when they're on the receiving end, but this eventually leads to frustration as they get fed up of your indecisiveness and lack of willingness to act or commit yourself. Passive people earn the reputation of being 'nicer', but they are just as irritating in the long term. Also, the harmful consequences on yourself can be just as great, if not worse. Passivity usually involves suppression of feelings, and you've seen how bad for you that can be. You can also end up being taken advantage of, and used as a 'doormat'.

How can I stop being so passive – it just comes naturally to me?
The following pages outline some ways. It isn't easy – none of this is, but if you concentrate on your behaviour, your feelings and self-confidence should start to become similar, making it easier for your desired behaviour to be achieved naturally.

DEALING WITH OTHERS' PASSIVITY

Just as when faced with aggression, when others are behaving passively towards us, we tend to **react** instinctively by being either aggressive or passive back. Choosing to **respond** assertively can be done with a little practice, however.

Reacting to passivity with passivity
This situation is extremely frustrating – neither party wanting to take responsibility or control, both trying to pass the issue to the other.

Reacting to passivity with aggression
This situation can arise when you become frustrated at the other person's continuing passivity, and become aggressive in an attempt to prompt them to action. It will often make you look bad, as the aggressor, and may make you guilty afterwards, as well as upsetting the passive person.

Responding to passivity with assertiveness – PLANT
Most people would agree that passivity is easier to deal with in the short term than aggression. It doesn't upset, anger or frustrate us nearly as much. So it may be easier to stay assertive.

Preparation
- If you're raising the issue, think how to set the scene and talk to the person in a way that doesn't threaten them. You need to think of ways to encourage them to have confidence, to talk and to say how they think and feel.

Listen
- Listen to what they have to say, and don't be afraid of silence. If they stop speaking without finishing what they have started to say, encourage them with something like, 'go on, I'm interested to know what you think'.

- Listen attentively, but don't put them under pressure. Remember, they may well be afraid of your reaction, so smile and try to appear reassuring. Make 'listening noises' like 'mmm', 'uh-huh', etc., and nod to encourage them.

Acknowledge
- Thank them for saying what they have said. It will encourage them to speak again.

- Acknowledge how they feel as well as what they have said. If they are very unsure of themselves, you can help them have confidence by saying something like, 'I really appreciate you talking to me about this – I know it isn't easy to do.' Some people will relate much better to you if they think you understand how they feel.

Now it's your turn
- Now state your own points, being firm but gentle – remember, they are afraid of your reaction, so try to be reassuring, without apologising or being passive.

Try to agree
- Passive people tend to anticipate not being listened to, or taken into account by others, so make sure you tell them you would like their agreement on what you decide **together**. Stress that their views *are* important.

- Try to leave the way open for them to talk to you again if they need to. Remember that to be really assertive, you need to end things so *they* feel good about themselves as well as you. So, even if you have said 'no' to them, try to think of something positive to

end on – like appreciating them taking the time to raise the issue
with you.

CHECKLIST

- Remember the viewpoint behind passive behaviour – that the
passive person feels 'less than' others. So encourage them to
develop confidence. Point out their good points, etc.

- Be aware that passivity only brings a temporary relief from an
unpleasant situation. The long-term effects are still unpleasant.

- Always be assertive and don't be tempted to get aggressive or
frustrated with passive people.

CASE STUDIES

Julia realises a member of staff is being taken advantage of
Julia prepared monthly rotas for the library staff. Most people were
content to work every other Saturday, but if something arose at
home, they exchanged duties. One week, she noticed that Marion,
one of the staff, was working on Saturday again.

'Marion, are you working Saturday for one of the others again?'
she asked. 'I think so,' Marion said, 'Angela was worried about
something her family had planned, and I don't have those
problems, living on my own, so I think I probably offered.'
'Sorry, Marion, did you offer to do it, or were you asked?' 'Well,
asked really, I suppose,' Marion said hesitantly, 'but I don't mind
really, it's always easy to change things round, and I don't like
letting people down.'

It was obvious that Marion had changed her own plans, rather
than say 'no' to one of the others who asked for help. Julia realised
that this had been going on for some time, and Marion wasn't likely
to change, but she wasn't happy about her being taken advantage of
all the time.

She made a decision that all rota changes were to be discussed by
both parties with her in future, not negotiated directly between staff.
Oddly enough, there were far fewer 'emergencies' needing rota
changes after that, and Marion seemed far more relaxed at work.
Passive people can easily be taken advantage of, as they don't like to
say 'no', for fear of the imaginary consequences.

Paul is frustrated by passivity in his brother

Paul's brother Adrian was going to be twenty-two on Sunday. Paul offered to take Adrian and his girlfriend out for the evening, with himself and his girlfriend. He asked Adrian to decide where he wanted to go.

By Saturday, when he came home from work, Paul still hadn't heard where they were going, so he called round to see Adrian. 'I'm not sure,' Adrian said, 'Where would you like to go?' 'It's your birthday, you choose!' said Paul irritably. He felt a little 'put out' that Adrian seemed so ungrateful. After all, the treat was likely to cost him a week's pay! 'I'm not sure, really,' Adrian replied. 'I'll ask Jackie tomorrow.' Paul felt that Adrian didn't really want to go anywhere at all. 'Don't bother,' he sniffed, 'I won't ask again!' and he left.

Adrian was bewildered. His reluctance to decide was due to his feeling that others' their views were more important than his own. But his behaviour irritated Paul, and made him feel unwanted as well as frustrated. In the end, Adrian avoided the short-term problem of upsetting anyone by making the wrong choice, only to cause another problem because Paul felt hurt. Passivity rarely solves problems in anything but the short term.

Erica struggles to choose some wallpaper

Erica wanted to have the spare bedroom decorated as a nursery, and her husband Martin agreed. They went to choose wallpaper. 'What do you think of this one?' Erica said, holding up a paper she had secretly fallen in love with. 'I don't know, what do you think?' Martin replied. 'Well, it's really nice,' Erica said, doubtfully – she didn't think Martin had sounded positive. 'Or do you think we should keep looking?'

Martin really liked the paper, but he wanted it to be Erica's choice. He interpreted her question as meaning that *she'd* rather keep looking, so he nodded. 'Yes, perhaps we should see the rest.' Erica was disappointed. They went to three more shops, but neither found anything they liked as much.

The problem with being passive and always putting others first is that they never find out what *you* want, so they can't help you. Also, they might not want to be put first – they might want you to decide for them. And most of all, when a passive person isn't sure what the other person wants, they try to work it out from the other person's tone of voice, expression, etc. – from intuition. And the problem with that is they may get it wrong, like Martin and Erica, and end up *not* pleasing the other person at all.

DISCUSSION POINTS

1. How many of the signs of passivity do you see in yourself? How do you think this affects your relationships with others?

2. Do you find it more difficult not to be passive with certain people? In certain situations? Use this to prepare yourself for times when you can predict it will be hard not to be passive.

3. How are you affected by others who are behaving passively? How can you help them to be more assertive?

7
Speaking Without Words

IDENTIFYING BODY LANGUAGE

We all communicate with people on three levels:

- What you actually say and hear – the **content** of the message.

- Unless you are blind or cannot see the other person (for example, when speaking on the telephone), there is also what you **see** – the visual signals the person gives out – the **manner** in which they give the message.

- Lastly, the interpretation and assumptions you make, based on the above – the **meaning** you perceive.

So the equation is:

$$\text{CONTENT} + \text{MANNER} = \text{MEANING}$$

Therefore, it isn't just enough to know *what* to say, you also need to be aware of the visual messages you give and receive. These visual messages are usually referred to as **body language**.

Understanding the importance of body language
It is important to understand body language for several reasons:

- You transmit and translate it instinctively, and usually not consciously.

- Because of this, it tends to be truer than the words you choose to use.

- Because of this, people tend to attach far more importance to speaker's body language than anyone realises. When someone is

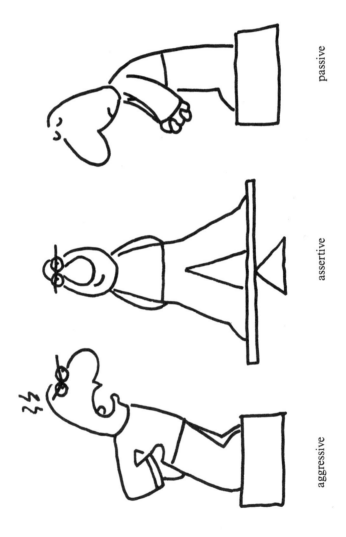

passive

assertive

aggressive

Fig. 5. Body language chart.

speaking to you, you gain only a fraction of the meaning from the words, and most of it from the body language.

So, if body language matches the words being said, no problem. However, if there is a difference, you usually interpret the message in line with the body language, not the actual words.

Below are some of the ways you can recognise aggressive and passive body language – the signs you can look for (see also Figure 5). Remember, if the words say one thing and the body another, it is the body you usually believe. Of course, it would be silly to think that just one or two of these signs indicates aggressive or passive behaviour, but looking at the whole picture, you can usually see many of the signs at once, which will enable you to judge their likely behaviour and viewpoint.

Recognising aggressive body language

Eye contact
- glaring
- staring

Facial expression
- chin forward
- gritting of teeth/jaw
- frowning
- narrowing of the eyes
- not smiling
- pale or red/purple face
- smiling sarcastically
- tight mouth

Movements and gestures
- bold, forceful movements
- finger pointing
- folded arms across chest
- head/face pushed forward

- striding about

- tapping – fingers, feet, etc.

- thumping fist

Positioning
invading your space – getting too close

looming over you

spreading out – taking up lots of space

Stance and posture
- leaning forward

- posed aggressively

Voice
- hard

- loud

- rises at end of sentences

- sarcastic

- uses much emphasis

- very firm

Recognising passive body language

Eye contact
- blinking often

- looking away/not meeting your eyes

- looking down

Facial expression
- changes rapidly

- pale or blushing

- raised eyebrows

- smiling nervously, or when obviously not happy

- wide eyes

Movements and gestures
- arms crossed low down (over stomach)
- covering hand with mouth
- jumpy movements
- nervous movements – shrugs, shuffles, fiddling, etc.
- shifting weight from foot to foot
- wringing hands

Positioning
- leaning back
- stepping back
- taking up as little space as possible

Stance and posture
- drooping shoulders
- keeping your distance
- tired, weary posture

Voice
- drops away at end of sentences
- dull
- monotone
- quiet
- soft
- whining
- wobbly

USING BODY LANGUAGE

So, what use are the signs? They can help you predict what someone's behaviour is likely to be. Also, you can learn to realise that their body language often (and usually) reflects how they feel, but what you really need to listen and respond to is their words. All too often, because we respond so strongly to body language, it causes us to **react**, and doesn't let us listen properly and choose how we want to **respond** to their message.

Responding to body language

You saw in earlier chapters that reactions tend to push you into behaviour that isn't always the best. So, you need to know how to respond to the body language.

1. Firstly, try not to react. Don't let someone's aggressive body language make you react aggressively or passively.

2. Using **PLANT**, acknowledge the body language as well as what they have said – the content. Say something like, 'I can see you're angry', or 'You're obviously uncomfortable about this', but remember not to use a patronising tone of voice, which could make things worse.

3. Acknowledging it may make the person reduce their body language. In turn, this will mean it has less effect on you, and you can respond more easily.

4. After acknowledging it, largely ignore it. Obviously if someone is very aggressive, make allowances for this and avoid getting them so angry they might lash out at you – keep your distance, but without backing off! Similarly, if someone is so passive that they are too afraid to communicate properly, make allowances for this and don't pressurise them too much – don't invade their space and crowd them.

5. Use assertive body language yourself, to try to bring them round to your viewpoint. This means treating them as equals, whether they are being aggressive or passive, and staying assertive. If their behaviour is making you feel non-assertive, then using assertive body language will help you stay confident and make it easier for you to think and speak assertively. If one person uses one sort of body language and another person another sort, one of the two people will usually start to change – to mimic the other. This is called **mirroring**. So, maintain body language yourself – let them mirror you, don't you mirror them!

6. You have read that body language is instinctive rather than conscious, as a rule. So you need to be aware of what assertive body language is, so you can keep your own body language in mind, and make sure you are looking assertive to match your words.

Recognising assertive body language

Eye contact
- good contact without staring

- looking at someone when talking to them or listening

Facial expression
- frowning when confused

- open, interested expression

- relaxed expression and jaw

- smiling genuinely

- steady expression

Movements and gestures
- head tilted when listening

- open gestures

- positive hand movements and gestures

Positioning
- appropriate distance between people

- leaning towards the other person

Stance and posture
- head held up

- relaxed

- upright, 'quietly confident', straight stance and posture

Voice
- clear

- firm

- sounds sincere

- steady

QUESTIONS AND ANSWERS

So, can I use body language to predict how a person will behave?
Yes. Remember that most people's body language is unconscious. Therefore, if they are showing body language of one behaviour, whatever they are saying, it is likely that they feel that way. They may be speaking calmly and logically, but if they are using aggressive body language, it is likely that they feel aggressive inside, so don't be surprised if they start to get 'wound up'.

If body language is unconscious, how can I choose to use assertive body language?
It is usually unconscious, and most people don't bother to think about it, unless they have had some training (such as management training, sales training, interpersonal skills training, or assertiveness training). But you *can* try to control your body language, and if you do this, it does two things. Firstly, it tends to take your mind off what *they* are doing, and focus your attention on what *you* are doing. This means you are responding, not reacting. Secondly, if you concentrate on looking assertive, it tends to make you feel and behave assertively as well.

Is body language really that important?
Yes. It is a fact that when two (or more) people are together, if one of them uses a certain body language, often the other will start to copy them – and similarly if one uses calm, assertive body language, the other may start to copy. This is known as **mirroring**, and you can use it to calm down situations, or to help passive people to 'open up' and have a little more confidence.

PROJECTING CONFIDENCE

Avoiding non-confident body language
Here are some of the common signs that indicate lying or dishonesty – behaviour that is *not* assertive and confident. If you wish to be seen as confident, you must avoid these.

Signs of lying or dishonesty
- avoiding eye contact

- covering the mouth when speaking

- frequent clearing of throat

- frequent wetting of lips

- looking down

- putting the hand on the throat

- rapid blinking

- repeated swallowing

- rubbing the eye, back of neck or nose

- scratching the head while speaking

- shrugging

- twitching.

Be significant

The more space you take up, the more you show others you are significant. This is why aggressive people take up a lot of space – it shows their 'better than' viewpoint. Passive people try to show they are 'less than' by taking up little space. It will show you are confident and feel that **you** are significant if you take up a reasonable amount of space, but you don't have to spread yourself out!

- Stand or sit tall, to use vertical space.

- Hold your arms away from your body – swing them slightly when walking, put a hand in a pocket when standing. When sitting, rest arms or elbows on the arms of chairs, put an arm on tables, etc.

- Stand with feet slightly apart.

Approach people

Aggressive people tend to crowd, while passive people shy away. Confident people are equal, so they don't need artificial spaces or barriers.

- Avoid crowding others.

- Don't stand behind barriers – desks, lecterns, tables etc., if giving a speech.

- Face people – don't stand facing another direction.

- Lean towards people.

- When people come towards you, step or lean towards them – meet them part-way.

- When sitting, clasp your hands in front of you and lean forward slightly on your elbows. Try making a steeple of your fingers in front of your chest – this also takes up some space and makes you more significant.

Be careful of movements

Aggressive people use hard, decisive gestures. Passive people use rapid, twitchy ones. Confidence is shown by people who use steady, measured movements.

- Keep your hands away from your face.

- Speak smoothly – not too fast or too slowly.

- Try to move smoothly, in a relaxed manner.

CHECKLIST

- Learn to identify the body language signs of aggressive and passive behaviour.

- Try to remember that these signs tend to make us react. They are the **manner** rather than the **content**. Accept them, but try not to react to them.

- Try to choose your response based on the content of the message, but allowing for the manner.

- Use assertive body language to help you respond not react, and to help you feel and behave assertively as well.

CASE STUDIES

Julia focuses on the content, not the manner

Julia had a very aggressive and angry customer. The lady came into the library complaining about the lack of parking facilities – she had waited 15 minutes for a parking space in the library car park. Julia dealt with her, and was very assertive.

Afterwards, the next customer commented, 'That was fantastic! I don't know how you kept your cool – I'd have punched her on the nose!' 'I felt like it!' Julia laughed, 'but to be quite honest, her comments were perfectly valid. We *are* a bit short of parking, especially on Saturdays when we're very busy.' The customer nodded. 'True, but that woman would still have got my back up!' he said.

Julia smiled, 'She *did* make me bristle at first, I must admit, but once I concentrated on the content of her message, and ignored the way she was delivering it – her manner – it made it much easier to keep calm.'

Paul breaks up a fight

One evening just after closing time, two customers started fighting outside the bar – not a serious fight, but a scuffle and lots of falling about and picking themselves up. Paul went out to sort it out as usual. He soon returned, having broken the pair up amicably.

'You're very good at that, aren't you?' his manager said. 'Thanks,' Paul said, 'it's just a knack, I suppose – trouble seems to evaporate once I put in an appearance!' What Paul didn't realise, which is a pity, is that he *is* actually quite skilful at using his body language in this sort of situation. He is very calm and keeps his hands in the open, making slow, steady gestures. Using calm, confident body language can sometimes calm others down – by encouraging 'mirroring'.

Erica's body language reveals her nervousness

Erica's boss arranged a meeting to try to settle a big contract, and several important people were due to come. Her boss was late from a previous appointment, and people started to arrive for the meeting before he returned. Erica made everyone coffee, and chatted to them while they were waiting, and they were all quite happy until she suddenly caught sight of her boss's car pulling into the car park.

Her heart sank, as he had often put her down in front of people, and she nervously started tidying the cups away, and shuffling papers. As she waited for him to come in, she started fiddling with her necklace and biting her lip – the guests saw her transformed before their very eyes into a nervous wreck! By the time her boss had come into the meeting room, the guests were also eyeing each other up nervously, and shuffling uncomfortably in their seats. Her boss started the meeting, but they were suspicious and reluctant to take him at his word.

It's surprising how much effect body language can have – people attach more importance to it than words, remember. People like Erica betray their true feelings, and broadcast their fears and hopes with body language.

DISCUSSION POINTS

1. Spend some time watching people you know. How do the assertive people use their body language? How do aggressive people and passive people behave?

2. Watch pairs of people together, for example in meetings, in a bar, or restaurant. Watch how they tend to mirror each other's body language – one copying the other. Think how you could use this to help others be more assertive.

8
Listening

Verbal communication needs three things to be successful – the message needs to be:

- spoken (broadcast)
- received
- and understood.

The biggest problem with listening is that it's hard to do. Listening properly isn't just something you do automatically, even though your ears are switched on all the time! The problem is that we can think about four times faster than we can speak – at least – some psychologists estimate it's even faster! Therefore, when someone is speaking, we can understand what they're saying in just a quarter of the available time, and we have three-quarters of the time to use our minds. So we have time to think about **other things** – not just what the speaker is saying. Sound familiar?

So we think about these other things, and if they happen to be more interesting or more time-consuming than we realised, suddenly before wc know it, we aren't listening any more. The mind doesn't keep up with what the other person is saying and we are no longer even giving the speaker the quarter of our thinking time necessary for listening. You need to listen **actively**.

LISTENING ACTIVELY

There are three reasons why you listen to people:

- self-interest – there's something in it for you
- interest in the other person
- your attention is grabbed by *how* they speak.

If any of these is applicable (or more than one), you will probably listen. However, the problem is that you can listen to something, but still not take it in, or not let the other person know you are listening. If you listen **actively**, it does several things:

- It makes you concentrate on listening, and not doing other things – it improves **reception** of the message.

- It gives the speaker confidence to speak – it improves the **broadcast**.

- As you are concentrating on listening, you are more likely to actually hear what is being said – it improves the **understanding**.

Why listen actively
As you read earlier, because you think about four times faster than you speak, there is a time delay between someone's speech and your mental thought processes when you are listening. What you do with the extra time your mind has to play with will govern how good a listener you are.

Some bad uses of the time lag for listeners
- Anticipating what will be said next, as this leads to . . .

- . . . finishing their sentences for them.

- Letting your mind drift onto something else.

- Mentally arguing with them – 'No it isn't', 'Rubbish!', etc.

- Mentally getting distracted by their looks, mannerisms, etc.

- Preparing the reply you will make when they have finished.

- Switching off – getting bored.

Good uses of the time lag
A better use of the time lag is to try asking yourself some of the following questions:

- Do they have a central theme or issue, and what is it?

- How are they making me feel, and is it relevant?

- Is there a way I can make this easier to remember?

- Is this fact or opinion?

- What are they *not* saying?

- What are they really trying to say?

- What can I deduce from their body language, tone of voice, etc.?

- What do they want from me?

- What evidence are they giving for their ideas/opinions, etc.?

Listening actively

☐ Ask questions to ensure you've understood them properly. This doesn't mean questioning their opinion or point, but questioning *your* understanding of it.

☐ Avoid anticipating what will be said next.

☐ Concentrate on what's being said.

☐ Don't interrupt.

☐ Look at them to show them they have your attention (but if they are nervous, remember to avoid gazing at them, as it may intimidate).

☐ Make gestures (e.g. nodding, smiling, etc.) and sounds (e.g. 'Uh-huh', 'Mmm', etc.) to show them you're listening.

☐ Stay open-minded, ready to change your own opinion if necessary.

IMPROVING YOUR LISTENING

Things to avoid

1. Allowing yourself to get distracted.

2. Being baffled by technical words and phrases. This is the one instance where you *can* interrupt – to say they need to explain the meaning of something before you can understand the rest of their message.

3. Being preoccupied with how you disagree with their facts/opinions.

4. Being too tired to pay attention properly.

5. Deciding in advance there's no point in listening.

6. External noises and distractions.

7. Getting excited or fascinated by what they're saying so much that your mind goes off at a tangent, and when you start listening again you've missed something.

8. Listening only for the bits you want to hear.

9. Reacting emotionally to specific words or phrases.

10. Switching off, because you think you know where they're going.

11. Switching off, because you think you're being given too much information – blanking it out.

12. Thinking of what you're going to say when it's your turn.

Improving your listening

1. Be interested in what's being said. Even if it doesn't sound interesting, it might turn out to be.

2. Be open-minded.

3. Concentrate on what's being said.

4. Help the speaker by nodding, smiling, etc.

5. Pay attention to their body language.

6. Remember not to interrupt until they pause, or invite you to speak.

7. Remember they have the right to express their thoughts/opinions even if you disagree.

8. Resist the temptation to anticipate.

9. Take notes if necessary.

QUESTIONS AND ANSWERS

So listening properly is about using the time delay properly?
Yes. Most people don't listen properly, not because of what their *ears* don't do, but because of what their *minds* do! Try to either keep your mind quiet, so you can listen, or use your mind to think of questions that will help you listen, as listed above under 'good uses of the time lag'.

What if I know they're wrong?
Keep quiet until they're finished. The next pages will show you how to deal with responding to others *after* you have listened to them. Don't interrupt. If the speaker is aggressive, they will probably respond with confrontation. If they're passive, they may get intimidated. Assertive people believe in equality, so let them finish before responding to what they've said. Think of it as a gift – you are giving them *your* time.

RESPONDING TO OTHERS

Checking and showing understanding
You can help both as a speaker and as a listener by learning how to **paraphrase**. Paraphrasing isn't repeating back exactly what someone said – that is parroting. Paraphrasing is summarising what was said **in your own words**. Paraphrasing does several things:

For the listener
• It calms angry speakers.

• It lets you clarify things you aren't clear about.

• It proves you received the message correctly.

For the speaker
• If people think you may ask them to paraphrase when you have finished, they tend to pay greater attention.

• It avoids misunderstandings.

• It lets you check their understanding.

Questioning

How not to ask questions
- Don't ask double-barrelled questions – 'Is it this or this?' They make people confused as to which part of the question to answer.

- Don't ask leading questions – 'Don't you think ...?' These tell the person the answer you expect, and they will usually either give it, or feel uncomfortable about disagreeing.

- Don't ask loaded questions – 'Why on earth did you ...?' These let the person know you feel a certain way about them and their actions – they feel judged.

- Don't ask long-winded, rambling questions. They can go off track and confuse people – they forget the beginning of the question, or don't realise exactly what you're asking.

- Don't ask multiple-choice questions – 'Is it this, or this, or that, or perhaps that?' They make people think they have to choose one of the offered answers, instead of thinking about an answer (which may have been better than one of the choices given). Also, they can make people feel they are being treated like an idiot. Finally, they also guess at one of the answers offered, so these questions don't really show understanding.

- Don't be ambiguous – asking questions that are confusing or have several meanings. It can lead to misunderstandings.

- Don't get carried away and ask a series of short, sharp questions. This will seem like an interrogation, and may make people feel defensive or threatened.

- Don't preface – saying first what *you* think, then asking *their* opinion. They will respond as with leading questions.

- Don't tack on little phrases to show the response you like – 'Isn't it?', 'Don't you?', etc.

Good ways to ask questions

- Ask open questions – these are ones that leave the response open to the other person, e.g. 'Tell me about...'. Other open questions are:

  How?

  What?

  When?

  Where?

  Who?

  Why?

Open questions are good because they usually give more information, and they allow the person more room to say whatever they need to say.

- Ask probing questions – 'Tell me more about...' or 'So why was that?' These sorts of questions also tend to include how, what, when, where, who and why.

- Ask one question at a time.

- Wait for a good time to ask a question.

- Wait for the answer before asking another question.

- Keep asking questions until you're satisfied with the answer.

CHECKLIST

- Listen actively – it concentrates your mind on the message and gives the speaker confidence – you are more likely to understand what they are saying.

- Use the time lag effectively – don't mis-use it!

- Avoid things that prevent you listening properly, and try to improve your listening.

- Check you have understood, and show understanding of other people's messages.

- Ask questions properly – both to ensure you've understood, and to check that others have understood you.

CASE STUDIES

Julia helps the children to listen

Julia's library held children's storytime sessions during the school holidays. Julia usually read these. One day, the children were particularly restless, because it was very hot and stuffy in the library. Julia adopted the technique of saying a few paragraphs of the story then asking questions: 'Why do you think he did that?', 'Do you think that will work?', 'Who knows what that means?' The children soon started paying more attention. By breaking the information up into small chunks, they only had to concentrate in small bursts, and the knowledge that they would be questioned gave them a motivation for listening. Listening became enjoyable, not a bore.

Paul's girlfriend feels she's not listened to

Paul's girlfriend came into the bar one evening while he was working, and sat at the bar, talking to him between customers. She was telling him about some new things she'd like to buy for their flat. Paul was listening to her, but also keeping an eye on a group of young lads who'd had a few too many drinks. He also kept serving customers, and was wiping down the bar when he wasn't actually serving.

Suddenly, his girlfriend went quiet. 'Forget it!' she said, 'And you can find somewhere else to live if you want to live in a pigsty! You never listen to a word I say!' And with that, she stormed out.

Paul was totally bewildered. He had been listening to every word, but hadn't *shown* her that he was – he hadn't listened *actively*. If he had said a few words of acknowledgement now and again, and perhaps nodded and looked at her a bit more, she would have realised he was listening.

Erica surprises her boss with some questions

Erica's boss is obviously a very unpleasant character. Erica often went to brief him about things that had happened while he was out or messages that she had taken, and he rarely even looked up, let alone acknowledged her words. One day, she'd had enough. She gave him three messages, then asked, 'So which would you like me to take care of first?' He paused, and said, 'Pardon?' 'I was wondering,' she said 'which would you like me to deal with first?' 'Does it matter?' he asked her. 'Probably not,' she replied, 'but I'd like you to decide in case I choose wrongly.' 'Reply to the lease company first, then the other two,' he said. She turned and walked out.

Her boss was probably baffled, but at least she had made sure she understood what was required. Perhaps if she asked questions more often, he would have less grounds to keep accusing her of being inefficient. After all, it's unfair of him to leave everything to her and then find fault with it. Using questions to check understanding can make sure you are doing things correctly.

DISCUSSION POINTS

1. Watch people having a conversation. What is their body language saying? Are they listening actively?

2. Think about when you are in conversations – are you using the time lag well. What do you tend to do with it? Is this a good use? How could you use it better to improve your listening?

9
Negotiating and Handling Change

NEGOTIATING

Everyone negotiates. Don't think you have to be settling some sort of deal or contract to be negotiating – it's just a word for coming to an agreement over something which you don't initially agree on. You negotiate every day over things like:

- children's bed-times

- how many times somebody does something

- the delivery date of something, e.g. furniture

- the price of something

- what to cook for dinner

- which television station to watch

- who will do a particular job or task.

The thing about negotiating is that when two or more people want different things, you tend to anticipate conflict. So you tend to behave as if you are expecting conflict. This isn't really a good start to negotiating – behaving as if you already disagree. You need to look at both points of view, and aim for a compromise you can both live with – exactly like assertiveness, the aim is that you both feel comfortable about the deal you strike.

There are five steps in negotiating:

1. Determining your own stance.

2. Finding out the other person's stance.

3. Looking for common ground.

4. Negotiating possible compromises.

5. Getting an agreement.

Figure 6 shows these in detail, and the rest of this chapter will explain each of the stages.

DETERMINING YOUR OWN STANCE

Why negotiating is difficult
Negotiating between people with different needs or viewpoints is difficult because:

- Each person has their own idea of what is best – their own self-interest.

- People often stick rigidly to their own position. If you do this, you can only succeed at the expense of the other person.

- People often think it's a loss of face to give in, and therefore see a compromise as failure on their part to win.

Determining your own requirements – your stance
Firstly, establish what you are trying to achieve, what you want, and what you need.

- What you want to achieve at the end of the day is your **objective**.

- How you would like to achieve that – in an ideal world – are your **wants**.

- What you **need** is something different again. Your needs are your minimum requirements.

Objectives
Imagine you are selling your car. Your objective would be:

1. To sell the car.

This sounds silly, but the objective is the real crux of the matter – why you are going to negotiate. Write it down, so you don't lose sight of it once you start discussing the issue. All the other details are not part of the objective – these will be dealt with in a minute.

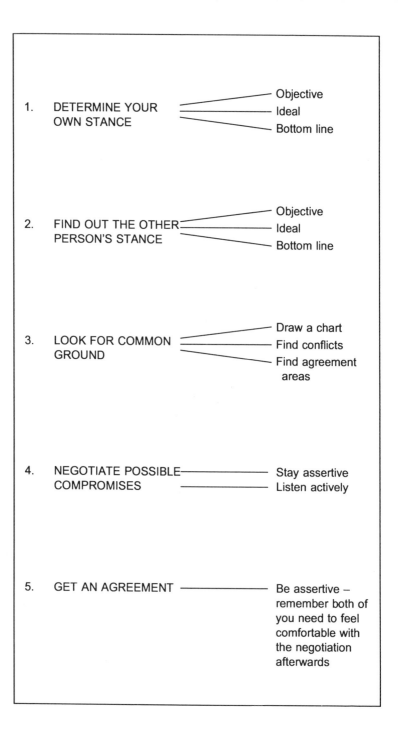

Fig. 6. Negotiating sequence.

Wants

Your wants are what you would *ideally* like – your ideal. Write these out as well. For the car example, these may be:

1. Sell the car quickly, before the new registration plate comes out in six weeks' time, and the car is a year more out of date.

2. Get the best possible price (as near as possible to the car's maximum valuation of £1,100).

3. Get paid in cash.

Your wants are your ideal. They may be vague – you don't have to be too specific unless you want to.

Needs

Now write down what you **need**. This can be very different from what you **want**. In the example, your needs may be:

1. Not sell for less than £750.

2. Get at least £250 in cash, the rest by cheque.

Can you see that your **wants** are your ideal – your optimum, whereas your **needs** are your minimum acceptable requirements – in negotiating terms your **bottom line**. Sometimes we refer to 'the ball park', or a 'ball park figure'. This basically means somewhere between the ideal and the bottom line.

You now know exactly what you are negotiating for – what you want, and what you need to achieve. You know your bottom line and ideal requirements, so you know the boundaries within which you can afford to be flexible – the ball park. Sometimes, this is referred to as your stance – or your position. It simply means where your boundaries are in relation to others. Figure 7 shows two different negotiating positions. If you imagine lines like this, you can easily see where the ball park is – it falls between the two bottom lines.

If it sounds complicated, try a simpler example. Suppose your friend wants you to go shopping with them, and you want to be back in time for an evening out. Your **objective** is to both go shopping with your friend, and then go out for the evening. Your **ideal** is to be back in time to get ready for the evening, without upsetting your friend. Your **bottom line** is to be home no later than

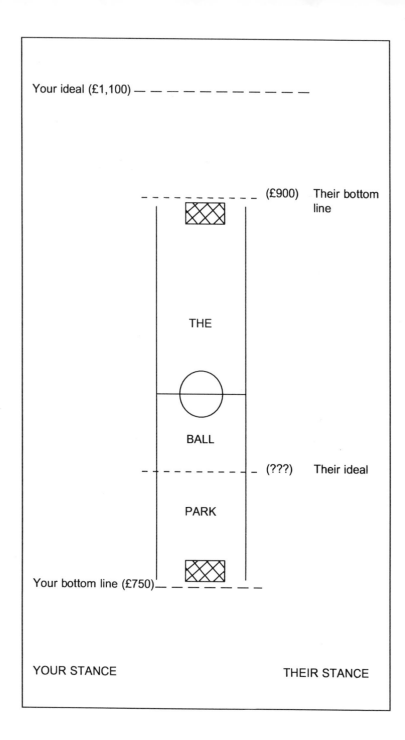

Fig. 7. Negotiating positions.

6.30, and for your friend also to leave by that time, so you can get ready. Perhaps you can now see that most people negotiate more than they think – often several times a day!

DETERMINING THE OTHER PERSON'S STANCE

The other person – the one you will be negotiating with – also has their own objectives, wants and needs. To negotiate properly, you really need to find out what these are, so you can see whether there is any point in negotiating at all. For example, if you want no less than £750 for your car, and he wants to pay no more than £700, there's no point in negotiating, because you can never come to a compromise.

Finding out information

You need to talk with the person, to try and find out these three things. Of course, they may well not tell you – after all, would you tell a potential buyer of your car that you want at least £750? Of course not – because then they wouldn't offer you any more! Similarly, they are unlikely to tell you the maximum price they can afford to pay – in case you put the price up. So sometimes you can use other methods of finding out, such as talking to other people to get their opinion of what the other person wants.

Staying with the car example, imagine the buyer's stance was this:

Objectives
1. Buy a car.

Wants
1. Pay as little as possible.

2. Get good value for money.

Needs
1. Not to spend more than £900.

2. Not to pay until after next payday (in two weeks' time).

LOOKING FOR COMMON GROUND AND GAINING AGREEMENT

Can you see from Figure 7 that you will never get your ideal in this example? Their bottom line is £900, and your ideal is £1,100, but anything over £900 is out of the ball park. So you are negotiating between a price of £900 and £750.

If you put all your information side by side in a chart, as in the example below, you can see where both parties correspond (see also Figure 7). This will give you a simple picture of where areas of conflict do indeed lie, and where they don't. If you aren't sure whether there will be a conflict or not, put a question mark. Don't worry about whether they are needs, wants or objectives, just try to match up the information where it relates to both people.

You can see from the chart that the only area of conflict you know about is the question of price – one of you will be negotiating towards as high a price as possible, the other towards as low a price as possible. The other areas are not necessarily a problem, unless

YOUR STANCE	THEIR STANCE	
To sell the car	To buy a car	✓
Sell the car quickly, before the new registration comes out in six weeks' time	Not to pay until payday (in two weeks)	✓
Get the best possible price	Pay as little as possible	✗
Get paid in cash		?
	Get good value for money	?
Not sell for less than £750	Not spend more than £900	✓
Get at least £250 in cash, the rest by cheque		?

more information comes to light. So where you have ticks you have possible compromises – you just have to agree the details. Where you have question marks you need to discuss things further, and where you have crosses you have potential conflict, and you need to iron these out first.

Building on common ground
One of the major tricks in negotiating is to build on the areas you have in common. This establishes constructive discussion, and makes an agreement much more likely.

Reaching an agreement

Do
- Remember the purpose of negotiating is to achieve a mutually acceptable outcome. This is often referred to as a 'win-win situation'.

- Make it easy for the other person to agree with you by thanking them and pointing out how co-operative they have been. This is not false flattery, you are acknowledging their assistance.

- Watch out for last-minute additional information, designed to 'throw a spanner in the works' and make you give in.

- Be ready to give a small concession to the other person if it helps sway them into agreeing. This is known as a 'sweetener'.

Don't
- Be reluctant to concede because you fear 'losing face'.

- Give in on a matter if it will only cause a similar future situation of conflict to arise – you are simply saving up problems, or creating new problems for the future.

QUESTIONS AND ANSWERS

So sometimes there's no point in even trying to negotiate?
Absolutely! If you look at the situation and the bottom lines mean there's no area between them (no ball park) then there's no way either of you will be able to reach an agreement unless one of you changes their bottom line.

Fig. 8. Reaction to change.

What if I can't find out what the other person's bottom line or ideal is?
This often happens – sometimes you have to make a sensible guess.
But if you use assertive communication, as explained in the earlier
chapters, combined with active listening, questioning correctly and
checking you understand exactly what they are saying, you should be
able to find out a surprising amount. And honesty often breeds
honesty – if you are a little open with them, they may reciprocate.
But remember, only give out a little information, in order to oil the
wheels of communication – don't blurt out too much, if it will
undermine your position by giving too much away.

COPING WITH CHANGE

Change is something that most people find difficult to deal with at
some time. Usually, we welcome changes that we are in control of,
such as buying a new car, moving house, changing job, etc. It's the
changes that are **imposed** on us by others that we find hard. Figure 8
shows the sequence of reactions which most people experience when
confronted with unwanted change.

Shock
This is the feeling of being overwhelmed by what is happening. You
may feel unable to react or think straight. If the change is a good,
welcome one, you may feel 'on cloud nine'.

How to cope
Find out as much as you can about the change. This will make it
seem more real. If you know what is happening, you can't go on to
the next stage, and deny it as easily.

Denial
You deny things are happening – it doesn't feel real. You may think
that the change won't affect you.

How to cope
Try to be part of things. Don't start thinking of yourself as being on
your own. See what others think – this will make it all seem more
real, and harder to deny.

Reaction
You realise the change *is* happening to you, and feel powerless to
stop it. This causes a reaction – you will usually react by doing

something (usually getting angry), or by doing nothing (usually getting depressed).

How to cope
Try to look at the potential benefits of the change – think positively. Concentrate on preparing for the change, don't just sit and wait. This can be hard if you aren't sure what's happening, or indeed, whether anything's going to happen at all, but plan for all eventualities. This will help you feel more prepared, and less likely to react by getting angry or depressed.

Letting go
You decide to let go of the past and accept that you are going to have to accept the change. This doesn't mean actually accepting it yet, just accepting that it *will* happen.

How to cope
You actually have to just come to terms with the fact that things can't always stay the way they are, and that the change will mean just what it says – change! If you find yourself longing for things to stay the same, try thinking of all the bad things about the old situation (and the opportunities which could be presented by the new situation), and this will help you think more positively about the new change.

Acceptance
This is where you finally accept the change and start to just let yourself experience it.

CHECKLIST

- Check your own stance before negotiating. You will communicate better if you know what you are trying to achieve.

- Always try to establish as much knowledge or awareness of the other person's stance as you can. This will avoid unnecessary negotiation that can't achieve anything.

- Look for areas of common ground to build on. This makes reaching an eventual agreement much more likely.

- Try to reach an agreement that is mutually acceptable. This may involve giving up part of what you want – you can't expect always to get your ideal.

- Accept that change may be inevitable, and you need to focus on how best to cope with it, not how to resist it.

CASE STUDIES

Julia negotiates her bottom line

Julia was at a management meeting, when the Area Librarian asked someone to do a particular report. Julia knew she had a small library, and therefore not many staff to cover for her if she spent a lot of time on research for the report. 'I'm sorry, but I'm not sure I have the time,' she said. 'I'm too busy,' said someone else. The third librarian said, 'I could do the research, but I'm on holiday in two weeks, so I couldn't actually write the thing, I'm afraid.' 'No,' said the Area Librarian, 'I want the same person to write the report as does the research, or it won't be done properly.'

Everyone's bottom line was that they couldn't do it. The only solution was for someone to change their bottom line, or there was no further point in trying to agree. 'Well,' said Julia, 'If David could cover my library for the next two weeks for, say, three days a week, instead of spending time doing the research, that would let *me* do the research. Then, I'll find time to do the report when he goes on leave.'

She had renegotiated her bottom line – her bottom line was 'no', unless circumstances changed. Don't get tied down by thinking your bottom line is set in concrete – it isn't. There's nothing wrong with changing other factors to change your bottom line.

Paul establishes clearly his bottom line

Paul was rostered for a day off one Wednesday, but the area manager scheduled an important meeting in the morning. 'I'm actually scheduled to be off that day,' Paul said, 'but provided we finish early, I'd be willing to come in.' 'I've already scheduled it for 10.30,' the manager said. 'Well, it *is* my day off, and I can't change it now,' Paul explained. 'If we could make an early start and finish by 10.30, I'd be happy with that.' 'No, it'll take too long,' said the manager. 'I'll get back to you if I can rearrange the date.'

Paul told his manager exactly what his bottom line was – no work after 10.30 on his day off. This meant that the manager could see straight away that there was no room to negotiate, because his meeting would take too long. He was therefore able to save both of them the time and effort of discussing it, choosing instead to reschedule.

Erica's mother struggles to cope with change

Erica's mother didn't want to be a grandmother yet. The prospect made her feel old, and every time Erica tried to involve her in shopping or planning for the baby, she said something like, 'Goodness, you've got ages yet to do all that – let's do it later, in a week or two.' Erica felt hurt, and thought her mother wasn't interested.

Her daughter being pregnant was a big change for Erica's mother, and in a way she was trying to deny that it was happening. As Erica grew larger, so the baby grew more real, and her mother would eventually come to accept it. Erica should have sat down and asked her mother what was wrong. If they had talked about how her mother felt, Erica would have seen that she wasn't meaning to hurt Erica's feelings, she just felt threatened.

On the sequence of response to change, Erica's mother was 'stuck' at the denial stage. She needed help to move on through the sequence, towards acceptance.

DISCUSSION POINTS

1. Think of a situation where you have negotiated over something that couldn't be resolved. What were the ideals and bottom lines of both sides? Was it ever going to be resolvable, or could you have negotiated a solution?

2. Think of an issue you need to work out with someone. Go through and establish your objective, ideal and bottom line. Then discuss things, and try to reach a workable solution.

3. Think of a change which has happened to you recently. Can you identify feeling each of the stages, even if briefly? How could you have moved through the sequence to acceptance quicker?

10
Staying Confident

Confidence is a feeling of being capable, being able to cope. The previous chapters will all help you feel more confident once you start applying what you have read. Here are some final hints on staying confident.

This chapter is slightly different from the others. The principles you read here will help you use the information in all the previous chapters to your best advantage.

USING TIMING TO BEST ADVANTAGE

Decide when

Choose when to deal with an issue. If you can't or don't want to deal with something now, say so, and schedule another time. This doesn't mean putting off things, which is called **procrastination**, and isn't helpful. What we mean here is not dealing with things when you aren't physically, emotionally or intellectually prepared. You aren't being unhelpful – it doesn't do anyone any favours to try to deal with something when you can't give it your best attention.

Example
Say something like, 'I *will* sort this out, but right now I'm too tired to think sensibly about it. I'm not avoiding the issue. Can we discuss it tomorrow morning, as I'll be better able to concentrate on getting it right then?' This reassures the person that you *aren't* putting them off, or procrastinating, and that you will do it, but not right now.

Don't be pressured

People often expect an instant answer to everything, but don't feel obliged to give one. There's another day tomorrow, and another week next week, so don't be pressured into something before you're ready. You have the right to time to think things over – an instant answer may well be incorrect, or not your real feelings.

Example

Just say something like 'I'm busy right now, can I have an hour to
think about it, and I'll get back to you?' You may be surprised how
many 'urgent' things that 'only you' can deal with have disappeared
by the time you get back to them – either that or someone else *could*
do it, after all!

Use timing to control what you deal with

Choose what issues to deal with, by picking your time. If you deal
with a problem at the time when it arises, it can sometimes make it
less important to people than if you deal with it separately.

Examples

Suppose you always drive home from social events, and you want to
have a break for a change. You have two real options:

1. deal with it next time the situation occurs, or
2. deal with it now, i.e. when the situation *isn't* occurring.

The danger of option one is that at the time, when people are
involved in the situation, they may not think clearly, rationally or
unemotionally. Saying 'Not this time' would be inconvenient,
unexpected and may seem petty and trivial. You are really only
saying 'no' to that one situation, and taking issue over something
you've never complained about before may seem trivial or even silly.
By taking option two, you speak to the people concerned about
what has happened in the past, and what you would like to happen
in the future – not about the present. Therefore, they can think more
clearly and sensibly. Also, they are then looking at the whole
situation, not just one instance of it.

   To give another example, suppose a friend or neighbour keeps
borrowing things because they have run out – coffee, milk, washing
powder. If you wait until next time they ask to borrow a pint of milk
to tackle them about it, what issue are you actually dealing with?
You're making a fuss about a pint of milk – petty, trivial and even
mean. Whereas, if you speak to them at another time, you're dealing
with the whole issue of their continual borrowing and how it affects
you.

TAKING RESPONSIBILITY

Own problems

When dealing with a problem, remember it's always your problem. The bottom line of this book has been that you can't change others, so you need to look at yourself and see how you can cope with others when they behave in ways you find difficult. This doesn't mean thinking everything's your fault – it isn't. What we're saying is that *they* may be causing the situation, but you can't control that, because you can't control them. What you can do is control your part in it. You *can* control yourself, and that's a lot to be able to control – a surprising amount.

Remember that 50 per cent of any situation (at least) rests with you. Forget the other 50 per cent. Work on what you *can* sort out – yourself. Do what you can, and hope it will have an effect on others. Don't say 'How can I stop him doing...', but 'How can I cope with him doing...'. At the end of the day, when there are two people in a situation, one of you has to change. Isn't it better to change yourself a little in a way you can control, rather than waiting for someone else to change, knowing they may never do it?

Example

You can't change people, so if someone is rude to you, for example, the problem isn't that they were rude, but that you didn't like it. Tell them how you feel, and how their behaviour affects you, but don't tell them how to behave – remember, you can't change people.

Say something like, 'When you speak to me like that, it makes me feel very upset and belittled. Please don't speak to me like that again.' Sounds simple, but try listening to people in the street and see how often they speak like that – not very often! Instead, you'll probably hear things like 'Don't do that! It makes me feel really small!' or 'What did you have to say that for? You know I don't like it!' It's completely different, isn't it?

Tell them what you *would* like, and point out how what you *don't* like makes you feel. Then focus your time and attention on coping with them and how they behave, not policing whether they behave better in future.

Let other people be

Other people can't be changed, so let them get on with their life. Be assertive, tell them how you feel, ask them to stop – all these things are good. But at the end of the day, if they don't change, that's up to them. Don't lose any sleep over it. Accept them the way they are.

Example
Suppose you have a friend whom you love dearly, but who embarrasses you in public, making silly rude comments to people. Childish, really, isn't it? You have three choices.

1. Ignore it. This may make you frustrated in the long term and eventually you may snap at them.

2. Say something and try to change them. This may frustrate you (and them) just as much if not more, if they don't change.

3. Say something and then let them be. They're grown up enough to make their own choices, so just tell them how you feel, then let them carry on. They may change, they may not, but it's up to them.

Be yourself
Just because you *can* be assertive, doesn't mean you *have* to. Be the way you want to be, within reason. There's a lot to be said for giving in occasionally to others, if you don't feel too strongly about something – it's called give and take. And there's also something to be said for letting your anger and aggression out sometimes. Some people need to be stood up to, just occasionally, to prevent them treating you as an inferior all the time. You don't always have to be assertive.

Tell the truth
If you know you are telling the truth, it gives you confidence. Always be honest if you can, but if it will save someone hurt and embarrassment, there's nothing wrong with a 'white lie' on an occasional basis – so long as you don't feel bad about it.

RESPECTING REALITY

Reality is relative. The facts about anything are only the facts as *you* know them, or as *you* see them. What is real to you may seem like a load of made-up rubbish to someone else. Just because you and someone else see the same thing differently, it doesn't mean that one of you has to be wrong. Look at Figure 9. Both people are looking at exactly the same thing. One person sees a beaker, one person sees a mug. Who's right? They both are, of course! But would you like to try to explain that to them? Of course not – they'd probably argue all day trying to prove one or other of them must be right, and therefore one or other of them must be wrong. The same applies to other problems.

Example
You go out with your friend, and they are rude to a shopkeeper. You are really embarrassed, and feel awful about how they have behaved. You tell them how you feel and they say 'No I didn't! I wasn't rude at all! And I'm sure she would have said something if I was!' Sound familiar? Well, maybe you're both right – remember the mug.

Fig. 9. Reality is relative.

You think your friend was rude because of what you saw, but they saw things from a different perspective. Arguing or discussing facts and how things happened can often be pointless. Facts are only facts from your point of view. And they can look different from a different perspective.

MANAGING YOURSELF

If you think about the principles in this chapter, and use the techniques and information in earlier chapters, you should be well on the way to being able to manage your own emotions, reactions and behaviour. Don't expect miracles – time and effort will make things easier as you go along, but at first things will seem impossible. The important thing is to make sure you don't get discouraged just because you try something and it doesn't work – or worse still, it makes things worse! Keep trying, and see how things go. Nobody's perfect – some of us just need more practice!

Glossary

Aggression. Behaviour coming from a viewpoint of being 'better than' others.

Assertiveness. Being aware of your own rights, needs and feelings, and expressing those appropriately to others, in a way that doesn't violate their rights, needs or feelings.

Ball park. The boundaries within which you can afford to be flexible.

Body language. The message you give out by means of your body – expressions, movements, stance, visual signals.

Bottom line. Your minimum requirements.

Copers. People with an inbuilt urge to cope with whatever life throws at them.

Drivers. Inbuilt standards we are driven to live our lives by.

Expression. Letting feelings out and behaving according to how you feel.

Hurriers. People with an inbuilt urge to hurry.

Mirroring. One person copying another person's body language – usually unconsciously.

Motive. Your reason for doing (or not doing) something.

Negative feelings assertion. Expressing how you feel, to avoid suppressing feelings.

Negotiating. The process of coming to an agreement about something.

Objective. What you want to achieve.

Passivity. Behaviour coming from a viewpoint of being 'less than' others.

Perfectionists. People with an inbuilt urge to be perfect.

Pleasers. People with an inbuilt urge to gain approval from others.

Procrastination. Putting off things until another time as a means of avoiding doing them now.

Reacting. Unconsciously behaving in a certain way as a result of events.

117

Responding. Choosing what you want to do – choosing your reaction.

Suppression. Bottling up feelings and behaving differently from how you feel.

Triers. People with an inbuilt urge to try hard.

Win-win. A mutually acceptable situation – acceptable to both parties.

Further Reading

Assertiveness at Work, Ken and Kate Back (McGraw-Hill 1982).
Dealing with Difficult People, Roberta Cave (Piatkus 1990).
How to Communicate at Work, Ann Dobson (How To Books 1995).
The Business of Assertiveness, Rennie Fritchie and Maggie Melling (BBC Books 1991).
How to Talk so People Listen, Sonya Hamlin (Thorsons 1988).
Teach Yourself Body Language, Gordon Wainwright (Teach Yourself Books 1985).

Index

HOW TO MASTER BOOK-KEEPING
A practical step-by-step guide

Peter Marshall

Illustrated at every stage with specimen entries, the book will be an ideal companion for students taking LCCI, RSA, BTEC, accountancy technician and similar courses at schools, colleges or training centres. Typical business transactions are used to illustrate all the essential theory, practice and skills required to be effective in a real business setting. 'Has a number of welcome and unusual features... The content is broken down into mind-sized chunks and the treatment is generally friendly.' *School Librarian journal.* 'An interesting approach.' *Association of Business Executives journal.* 'A complete step-by-step guide...each section of the book teaches a useful skill in its own right.' *OwnBase.* 'In addition to providing a useful approach to the teaching and learning of book-keeping skills, the way in which the text is presented should ensure that the book also provides a valuable reference source for revision and prompting.' *Teeline.*

176pp illus. 1 85703 065 6. 2nd edition.

WRITING BUSINESS LETTERS
A practical introduction for everyone

Ann Dobson

Without proper help, lots of people find it quite hard to cope with even basic business correspondence. Intended for absolute beginners, this book uses fictional characters in a typical business setting to contrast the right and wrong ways to go about things. Taking nothing for granted, the book shows how to plan a letter, how to write and present it, how to deal with requests, how to write and answer complaints, standard letters, personal letters, job applications, letters overseas, and a variety of routine and tricky letters. Good, bad and middling examples are used, to help beginners see for themselves the right and wrong ways of doing things. Ann Dobson is principal of a secretarial training school with long experience of helping people improve their business skills.

183pp illus. 1 85703 339 6. 2nd edition.

HOW TO MANAGE PEOPLE AT WORK
A practical guide to effective leadership

John Humphries

'These days, if a textbook on people management is to succeed, it must be highly informative, reliable, comprehensive – and eminently user-friendly. Without doubt, *How to Manage People at Work* is one such book. Written in an attractive style that should appeal to any first-line manager who has neither the time nor the energy to cope with heavy reading, John Humphries has tackled his extremely wide subject ably and well. Rightly or wrongly, it has always been my experience that one has only to read the first couple of pages of any textbook on people management to discover whether or not the author enjoys an empathy with the people at the sharp end – and here is one author who, for my money, has passed the test with flying colours.' *Progress/NEBS Management Association.*

160pp illus.1 85703 068 0. 2nd edition.

HOW TO MASTER PUBLIC SPEAKING
A handbook for every occasion

Anne Nicholls

Speaking well in public is one of the most useful skills any of us can acquire. Whether you are a nervous novice or a practised pro, this step-by-step handbook tells you everything you need to know to master this highly prized communication skill. 'In addition to usefulness of content, the book has attractiveness of print, paper and binding to recommend it.' *Spoken English.* 'I found this book an excellent read and recommend it wholeheartedly. It is full of helpful practical information.' *Phoenix/ Association of Graduate Careers Advisory Services.* 'Especially welcome is the constant stress on the needs of the audience being of paramount importance... A good deal to recommend it.' *Speech & Drama.*

160pp illus. 1 85703 149 0. 3rd edition.

WINNING PRESENTATIONS
How to sell your ideas and yourself

Ghassan Hasbani

'Good communication skills' is a phrase repeatedly used in job descriptions and CVs. These skills can make or break people's careers and are highly regarded by employers and organisations. One of the most important skills is the ability to present and put your ideas across whether you are an employee or an independent consultant, a civil servant or businessperson, a school teacher or a university lecturer, a member of the local club or someone starting a career in politics. No matter who you are or what kind of work you do, you always need to communicate with people on different occasions and present to them ideas, news, or achievements. This step-by-step guide tells you all you need to know in order to become confident in giving effective presentations, that will help you succeed in your life and career. Presenting is not necessarily a gift, it is a skill which can be learned or acquired and this book will help you do that. Ghassan Hasbani started writing and presenting for television at the age of 16. He currently works as a telecommunications engineer, where he uses his skills to present new technologies in seminars and lectures. He also works as a visiting university lecturer teaching management and communication skills to undergraduates.

160pp illus. 1 85703 304 3.

HOW TO MANAGE AN OFFICE
Creating and managing a successful workplace

Ann Dobson

Good office management is one of the keys to success in any organisation. The benefits are a happy and productive staff, satisfied customers, and a sound base from which to tackle such issues as growth and change within the organisation. Written by an experienced office manager and business consultant, this book suggests a complete practical framework for the well run office. It discusses what the office is for, the office as communications, the office as workplace, equipment, hygiene, health and security, external appearances, managing visitors, handling orders and information, managing office supplies, the office budget, staff management, and managing an office move.

160pp illus. 1 85703 049 4.

HOW TO EMPLOY & MANAGE STAFF
A practical handbook for managers and supervisors

Wendy Wyatt

Now in a revised second edition, this easy to use handbook is intended for all young managers, supervisors and students whose work will involve them in recruiting and managing staff. Ideal for quick reference, it provides a ready-made framework of modern employment practice from recruitment onwards. It provides a clear account of how to apply the health & safety at work regulations, how to handle record-keeping, staff development, grievance and disciplinary procedures, maternity and sick leave and similar matters for the benefit of the organisation and its employees. The book includes a useful summary of current employment legislation and is complete with a range of model forms, letters, notices and similar documents. Wendy Wyatt MIPD is a Personnel Management and Employment Consultant; her other books include *Recruiting Success* and *Jobhunt*.

176pp illus. 1 85703 167 9. 2nd edition.

HOW TO COMMUNICATE AT WORK
Making a success of your working relationships

Ann Dobson

Things only get done properly at work if everyone communicates effectively – whatever their individual role in the organisation. This very practical step-by-step guide gets to the very basics of good communication – what it is and why we need it, how to speak and listen, how to ask and answer questions, how to take messages and use the telephone; how to liaise, negotiate, persuade, offer advice and accept criticism; how to stand up for yourself, dealing with shyness, a difficult boss or angry customer; how to use and understand body language properly, how to cope with visitors, how to store and present information, how to use the English language correctly – and a great deal more, illustrated throughout with examples and case studies. Written by an experienced office staff trainer this book will be a real help to all young people starting a new job, or older individuals returning to work after time away.

192pp illus. 1 85703 103 2.

How To Books

How To Books provide practical help on a large range of topics. They are available through all good bookshops or can be ordered direct from the distributors. Just tick the titles you want and complete the form on the following page.

___ Apply to an Industrial Tribunal (£7.99)
___ Applying for a Job (£7.99)
___ Applying for a United States Visa (£15.99)
___ Be a Freelance Journalist (£8.99)
___ Be a Freelance Secretary (£8.99)
___ Be a Local Councillor (£8.99)
___ Be an Effective School Governor (£9.99)
___ Become a Freelance Sales Agent (£9.99)
___ Become an Au Pair (£8.99)
___ Buy & Run a Shop (£8.99)
___ Buy & Run a Small Hotel (£8.99)
___ Cash from your Computer (£9.99)
___ Career Planning for Women (£8.99)
___ Choosing a Nursing Home (£8.99)
___ Claim State Benefits (£9.99)
___ Communicate at Work (£7.99)
___ Conduct Staff Appraisals (£7.99)
___ Conducting Effective Interviews (£8.99)
___ Copyright & Law for Writers (£8.99)
___ Counsel People at Work (£7.99)
___ Creating a Twist in the Tale (£8.99)
___ Creative Writing (£9.99)
___ Critical Thinking for Students (£8.99)
___ Do Voluntary Work Abroad (£8.99)
___ Do Your Own Advertising (£8.99)
___ Do Your Own PR (£8.99)
___ Doing Business Abroad (£9.99)
___ Emigrate (£9.99)
___ Employ & Manage Staff (£8.99)
___ Find Temporary Work Abroad (£8.99)
___ Finding a Job in Canada (£9.99)
___ Finding a Job in Computers (£8.99)
___ Finding a Job in New Zealand (£9.99)
___ Finding a Job with a Future (£8.99)
___ Finding Work Overseas (£9.99)
___ Freelance DJ-ing (£8.99)
___ Get a Job Abroad (£10.99)
___ Get a Job in America (£9.99)
___ Get a Job in Australia (£9.99)
___ Get a Job in Europe (£9.99)
___ Get a Job in France (£9.99)
___ Get a Job in Germany (£9.99)
___ Get a Job in Hotels and Catering (£8.99)
___ Get a Job in Travel & Tourism (£8.99)
___ Get into Films & TV (£8.99)
___ Get into Radio (£8.99)
___ Get That Job (£6.99)
___ Getting your First Job (£8.99)
___ Going to University (£8.99)
___ Helping your Child to Read (£8.99)
___ Investing in People (£8.99)
___ Invest in Stocks & Shares (£8.99)

___ Keep Business Accounts (£7.99)
___ Know Your Rights at Work (£8.99)
___ Know Your Rights: Teachers (£6.99)
___ Live & Work in America (£9.99)
___ Live & Work in Australia (£12.99)
___ Live & Work in Germany (£9.99)
___ Live & Work in Greece (£9.99)
___ Live & Work in Italy (£8.99)
___ Live & Work in New Zealand (£9.99)
___ Live & Work in Portugal (£9.99)
___ Live & Work in Spain (£7.99)
___ Live & Work in the Gulf (£9.99)
___ Living & Working in Britain (£8.99)
___ Living & Working in China (£9.99)
___ Living & Working in Hong Kong (£10.99)
___ Living & Working in Israel (£10.99)
___ Living & Working in Japan (£8.99)
___ Living & Working in Saudi Arabia (£12.99)
___ Living & Working in the Netherlands (£9.99)
___ Lose Weight & Keep Fit (£6.99)
___ Make a Wedding Speech (£7.99)
___ Making a Complaint (£8.99)
___ Manage a Sales Team (£8.99)
___ Manage an Office (£8.99)
___ Manage Computers at Work (£8.99)
___ Manage People at Work (£8.99)
___ Manage Your Career (£8.99)
___ Managing Budgets & Cash Flows (£9.99)
___ Managing Meetings (£8.99)
___ Managing Your Personal Finances (£8.99)
___ Market Yourself (£8.99)
___ Master Book-Keeping (£8.99)
___ Mastering Business English (£8.99)
___ Master GCSE Accounts (£8.99)
___ Master Languages (£8.99)
___ Master Public Speaking (£8.99)
___ Obtaining Visas & Work Permits (£9.99)
___ Organising Effective Training (£9.99)
___ Pass Exams Without Anxiety (£7.99)
___ Pass That Interview (£6.99)
___ Plan a Wedding (£7.99)
___ Prepare a Business Plan (£8.99)
___ Publish a Book (£9.99)
___ Publish a Newsletter (£9.99)
___ Raise Funds & Sponsorship (£7.99)
___ Rent & Buy Property in France (£9.99)
___ Rent & Buy Property in Italy (£9.99)
___ Retire Abroad (£8.99)
___ Return to Work (£7.99)
___ Run a Local Campaign (£6.99)
___ Run a Voluntary Group (£8.99)
___ Sell Your Business (£9.99)

___ Selling into Japan (£14.99)
___ Setting up Home in Florida (£9.99)
___ Spend a Year Abroad (£8.99)
___ Start a Business from Home (£7.99)
___ Start a New Career (£6.99)
___ Starting to Manage (£8.99)
___ Starting to Write (£8.99)
___ Start Word Processing (£8.99)
___ Start Your Own Business (£8.99)
___ Study Abroad (£8.99)
___ Study & Learn (£7.99)
___ Study & Live in Britain (£7.99)
___ Studying at University (£8.99)
___ Studying for a Degree (£8.99)
___ Successful Grandparenting (£8.99)
___ Successful Mail Order Marketing (£9.99)
___ Successful Single Parenting (£8.99)
___ Survive at College (£4.99)
___ Survive Divorce (£8.99)
___ Surviving Redundancy (£8.99)
___ Take Care of Your Heart (£5.99)
___ Taking in Students (£8.99)
___ Taking on Staff (£8.99)
___ Taking Your A-Levels (£8.99)
___ Teach Abroad (£8.99)
___ Teach Adults (£8.99)
___ Teaching Someone to Drive (£8.99)
___ Travel Round the World (£8.99)
___ Use a Library (£6.99)

___ Use the Internet (£9.99)
___ Winning Consumer Competitions (£8.99)
___ Winning Presentations (£8.99)
___ Work from Home (£8.99)
___ Work in an Office (£7.99)
___ Work in Retail (£8.99)
___ Work with Dogs (£8.99)
___ Working Abroad (£14.99)
___ Working as a Holiday Rep (£9.99)
___ Working in Japan (£10.99)
___ Working in Photography (£8.99)
___ Working in the Gulf (£10.99)
___ Working on Contract Worldwide (£9.99)
___ Working on Cruise Ships (£9.99)
___ Write a CV that Works (£7.99)
___ Write a Press Release (£9.99)
___ Write a Report (£8.99)
___ Write an Assignment (£8.99)
___ Write an Essay (£7.99)
___ Write & Sell Computer Software (£9.99)
___ Write Business Letters (£8.99)
___ Write for Publication (£8.99)
___ Write for Television (£8.99)
___ Write Your Dissertation (£8.99)
___ Writing a Non Fiction Book (£8.99)
___ Writing & Selling a Novel (£8.99)
___ Writing & Selling Short Stories (£8.99)
___ Writing Reviews (£8.99)
___ Your Own Business in Europe (£12.99)

To: Plymbridge Distributors Ltd, Plymbridge House, Estover Road, Plymouth PL6 7PZ. Customer Services Tel: (01752) 202301. Fax: (01752) 202331.

Please send me copies of the titles I have indicated. Please add postage & packing (UK £1, Europe including Eire, £2, World £3 airmail).

☐ I enclose cheque/PO payable to Plymbridge Distributors Ltd for £ _____

☐ Please charge to my ☐ MasterCard, ☐ Visa, ☐ AMEX card.

Account No. ☐☐☐☐☐☐☐☐☐☐☐☐☐☐☐☐

Card Expiry Date ☐☐ 19 ☎ **Credit Card orders may be faxed or phoned.**

Customer Name (CAPITALS) ....

Address ....

.... Postcode ....

Telephone .... Signature ....

Every effort will be made to despatch your copy as soon as possible but to avoid possible disappointment please allow up to 21 days for despatch time (42 days if overseas). Prices and availability are subject to change without notice.

Code BPA